DIGITAL
PRESIDENT

WHY SOME FUNNELS
CREATE AUTHORITY | ATTRACT AUDIENCES
CONVERT CUSTOMERS | BUILD COMMUNITIES
AND OTHERS DON'T

BY

MICHAEL REESE & WOODS DAVIS

DIGITAL PRESIDENT
Why Some Funnels Create Authority, Attract Audiences,
Convert Customers, Build Communities and Others Don't.

Hardcover ISBN: 978-0-692-97646-3
Paperback ISBN: 978-0-692-94423-3

Cover design: Digital President LLC
Editing and Interior Layout: Digital President LLC

DEDICATION

———

This book is dedicated to the future Digital Presidents who are committed to bringing value to the world and know there's a better way to do it.

CONTENTS

ACKNOWLEDGMENTS

We have so many great friends, partners and clients who have contributed to the creation of this book. They are all wonderful and have had a hand, one way or another, in making this book possible. Please know how grateful we are for your input, expertise and support while we worked to make *Digital President* a reality.

Anna & Blair Davis, Cache, Cort & Crew Reese, Clate Mask, Emily Wydeven, Eric Isaksen, Hal Elrod, Hubspot, Jay Abraham, Kelly Edwards, Marc Chesley, Stacy Reese, Wally Bressler, Whitney Davis

FOREWARD BY JAY ABRAHAM

——

My life has been defined by working in 465 industries, not businesses. I got a very clear understanding of how much more was possible when I started seeing that people in one industry don't have a clue what people in another, and another, and another think. They don't understand the strategy, the revenue streams, the selling approaches, the access vehicles, the lead generation, conversion. But then I got the great pleasure of having three different activities in my life which transformed my thinking.

The first was when I worked for the largest international multi-variable testing organization in the world. They spent billions of dollars with clients at big corporations to experimentally compare and test the performance of all kinds of different ways of doing things. In manufacturing, they checked different ways of operating a line, different ways of producing products for efficiency, for consistency, for quality, for minimizing breakdowns, maintenance, etc.

In the selling arena, they tested everything from different ways of greeting people at the front door at the store, different ways of starting a relationship when you're calling cold, the different ways of multi-stage selling, which is a type of selling where you don't close on the first call. The different ways of merchandising in retail, different places you put different numbers of SKU's, maybe six bottles instead of four, and so on. They found that changing one variable can transform the result of something as much as 300%.

Then I went into a very immersive experience in direct response. Direct response is very self-explanatory, and it's what every entrepreneur should be doing. Everything you do should be generating a direct and immediate response; a response that is measurable is quantifiable and that is bite-sizable in a certain, projected way. When you're doing direct response, you get the education of a lifetime, and you also get the shock and stun of a lifetime; because you realize that by changing one element, like changing a headline, you can improve or suppress the result as much as 21 times. You have changed the proposition or the positioning, which can improve or suppress the result up to 5 times or 500 percent. Change the credibility factor, you could improve or suppress the results. I could go down a litany of these things.

When you see the power of these elements, and then, when you see the combination of improving not one, but the three, five, ten of these elements you see how companies that do it double, and redouble, and redouble again their performance. You actually hurt in your heart for people who accept status-quo, for people who don't understand highest and best use.

You can harness these principles in the digital space for exponential growth.

Michael has been a fanatical student of my work for 15 years.
Michael and Woods have taken my work and applied it both impressively and qualitatively to the digital marketing space in a way few other entrepreneurs understand. There is no one I know that would not benefit from both reading their work and implementing their strategies. Worst case, your mind will grow. Best case, your business will grow and outsize your competitors.

You have to look at every element of your performance in your professional life and judge it as if it was a portfolio. It is a portfolio of integrated activities and actions that collectively represent your career, your success and the asset which is really the brand and the value that you are building perpetually.

A book can be a cornerstone of your brand. The cost of 5,000 books is minimal but the value of 5,000 devotees multiplied by referrals can own a market.

Most people that are teaching my book strategy or how to write a book, or how to publish a book, are abusing the people because they produce books that offer no meaning, quality, and actionability besides just being a calling card and a perceived differentiator. I offer this trust-based endorsement of Digital President because Michael and Woods advocate integrity and superior value above and beyond all the low quality, insubstantial information I've seen others teaching online.

This book is instructional not motivational. It shows you how much more you can achieve for yourself with higher performing strategies, actions, thinking, self-vision, and understanding of the forces, power, and actions that exist in the marketplace, and the alternatives that are available. When you see the same time, the same effort, the same money, the same interaction, the same communication, the same ads, the same emails, can communicate something to produce multiple times the result, you do get motivated, because you see how much more is possible.

- Jay Abraham

Jay Abraham is the world's preeminent business growth expert. So far, he has helped clients generate over $21.7 billion dollars in capital increases across hundreds of industries. He is a legend in entrepreneurship circles and mammoth-force in original thinking. For more information about Jay visit: www.Abraham.com

INTRODUCTION

—

"Don't set out to build a wall. You don't say, 'I'm going to build the biggest, baddest, greatest wall that's ever been built.' Don't start there. You say, 'I'm going to lay this brick as perfectly as a brick can be laid.' Do that every single day and soon you have a wall."

—Will Smith

In the first 90 days after we launched our book, we were able to drop our cost to acquire a client online from $10.80 to $0.79. The number of leads we used to generate monthly for a cost of $5,500, we were now able to get for only $400. It was a game changer for us not just because of the 92 percent reduction in cost, but also because it was the result of a completely predictable client acquisition strategy.

After 10 years of selling online and bringing in $45 million in revenue from our efforts, we created the predictable strategy that is now known as the "Community Funnel."

When we say Community Funnel, we mean that by doing the right things in the right order, you can create a single, killer funnel that provides leverage for you in your sales and marketing efforts so you can create automatic, predictable income without investing a significant amount of your own time and resources to make sales.

How we arrived at this reality was not a mistake; it was the result of years of testing and learning the fundamental differences between advertising and marketing. As with all successful marketing, getting a clearer understanding of the client's perspective, and understanding that they are on a journey, helped us align our efforts and engagement with our audience as they moved through the stages of making a buying decision.

At the core of this was a mindset change; it was the application of being preeminent with all of our communication and engagement.

Here's how we knew we nailed it.

We've had success on multiple occasions where we'd built an online marketing funnel and turned it into real money by driving significant Monthly Recurring Revenue (MRR). In fact, over the past 12 months, we were able to generate MRR of over $400,000 on two different ventures.

On one of those occasions, we even achieved $450,000 in MRR in only six months. To say that we did it without any challenges, however, would be a lie.

From the outside looking in, it appeared that everything we touched turned into gold. One of my friends who has a Harvard MBA, and is a 3-D chess player when it comes to business, refers to our unique abilities to sell online as the "*yes gun.*" He calls it that because we know how to get the attention of the audience we want, and more importantly, we know how to get people to say: "Yes."

Despite all the praise and success, as we took a closer look, we realized that things weren't exactly as they should be.

After doing some mental gymnastics around it, we came to the conclusion fairly quickly that not all revenue is equal. Sure, it's great to have money coming in, but that doesn't mean everything is perfect.

In other words, "Mo' money, mo' problems."

Success is as Hard to Navigate as Failure

With each new idea that we turned into a business, we always learned some great lessons. These lessons caused us to spend time thinking about what we would do differently and what questions we should have asked along the way … even before we put the idea in motion.

Each opportunity requires a different sacrifice of both time and resources. Each idea we worked with had different trade-offs with varying levels of give and take from both of us and from anyone else involved in the process.

From our perspective, success is just as hard to navigate as failure, and we think this quote from Stephen R. Covey sums it up best: "If the ladder is not leaning against the right wall, every step we take just gets us to the wrong place faster."

We say this, because at times, we had the ladder up against the wrong wall ourselves.

In some of the marketing strategies we employed, we didn't fully take into consideration the secondary impact and effect of each decision we were making. Sometimes, we even skipped several steps that turned great business ideas into terrible businesses.

For example, one of our best ideas was a great concept, but we were servicing the wrong segment of the market. The value proposition we created, combined with the wrong business model, translated into a lot of clients that were not ideal for our business.

Yes, we got off to a fast start, with a lot of people buying our product, which resulted in us generating some great revenue. If getting someone to buy was an Olympic event, we were triple gold medalists. As well, if the only goal was to generate revenue, we were clearly winning. But as we mentioned earlier, all revenue is not equal. Plus, while it was great to have customers and revenue, we weren't really getting any fulfillment from what we were doing.

"Success without fulfillment is the ultimate failure."—Tony Robbins

As we looked at this most recent edition of our business model, we came to the conclusion that if we spent more time with the same energy and effort on the front end, being strategic in our approach, we could create a more predictable, scalable, and profitable business.

Taking this angle to solving our problem played nicely into a Core Philosophy we share: problem solving. We've borrowed some of the best mental models from the smartest people in the world like Elon Musk. When it comes to problem solving, we simply boil things down to their fundamental truths then reason up from there. Every problem has a solution. We are always in search of finding a better way. We want to consider all the possible solutions—said differently—"What are all the ways to accomplish the goal?"

What we discovered by thinking and working this way was that although our clients had money to make an initial purchase, they didn't have enough money to make subsequent or ancillary purchases to get the most out of our product. We were selling a product and servicing clients in a flat to declining opportunity.

What we also concluded was that our fulfilment came from creating products that added value to our Ideal Clients: people that not only had money, but people that we love spending time with.
Seeing this, we made the hard decision to sunset the product that served the wrong market. At the same time, we realized that we needed a strategy that would help us fix the known problems—something with a really high margin that would take few to no resources.

And most importantly, we needed it to be dependable and predictable.

The Community Funnel Strategy

To solve the problem, we had to define our target market and the different "buyer personas" we were going to serve. With our new mindset, we wanted to really understand the different situations of each persona. Doing this would allow us to be more relevant, resulting in a better way to create value that would ultimately result in building stronger trust, better conversions, and shorter sales cycles.

We made a list of all the situations and the solutions we could provide. Then, we leveraged the mental models from the book *Change Your Questions, Change Your Life*; we started question-storming everything from the perspective of each persona, then aligned those answers to our strategy of delivering value.

We asked questions like:

- What was the best top-of-funnel strategy we ever leveraged that produced the desired outcome?
- Should the top of funnel address problems, or solutions?
- Where was the intersection of our expertise and knowledge that creates our greatest market opportunity?
- What information do we need to know about our subscribers in order to best communicate?
- What was the real goal?
- What was each persona's desired outcome?
- What things have we been doing that are actually moving us further away from the goal?
- What things should we start doing that we're not doing?
- What things should we stop doing that we are doing?

We believe the strategist always wins, and at the heart of a bad strategy is solving the wrong problem.

By asking these questions, we were thinking strategically to determine what the exact problem was so we could solve it. As we asked ourselves these questions, one question that kept coming up that gave us a great frame of reference was: "If we started from scratch today, knowing what we now know, what would be the best solution for our problem?"

The answer: The only funnel anyone would ever need if done correctly was The Community Funnel.

The Community Funnel leverages marketing principles like value proposition, direct response, content marketing, influence, automation, upsells, downsells, self-liquidating offers, guarantees, risk reversals, positioning, authority, minimal viable products, and most importantly, product-market fit.

Instead of just advertising and pitching your product or service, the Community Funnel provides relevant, valuable content to solve your prospect's issues at every stage of the Buyer Journey—increasing trust and ultimately culminating in a decision to buy from you. It leverages a proven model for content creation and distribution that anyone can employ to create the perfect Buyer Journey resulting in predictable, automated income.

In the past, we skipped so many of the important elements of building a relationship marketing and sales funnel. Like many other marketers, we skipped steps because we wanted to make money fast.

Unfortunately, 80 percent of businesses that fail, fail because of poor sales and marketing. They don't focus on perfecting the Buyer Journey; they only focus on people who are ready to do business now.

You see, when you concentrate only on sales and marketing, you neglect to address the fact that a majority of the people who are "interested," or considering making a buying decision, are not ready to buy. Knowing this, your communication to these people should be segmented not only by who they are, but also by where they are in the process.

We call this "The Buyer's Majority Principle."

We were determined to not let that happen ever again. So we created a system with a checklist so we could make sure that every time we launched a new product, idea, or business—it would be an absolute hit.

As we worked on our next product, we documented the goal of each step and what questions to ask ourselves.

Some of the questions we asked ourselves were:

- What were we really good at?
- What problems could we solve in the marketplace?
- What was the Ideal Client willing to pay to have that problem solved?
- What was our target market?
- Who were the different buyer personas we would serve?
- What is the promise we are making to that client?
- How much time will be needed to fulfill the promise?

We took the time to deconstruct every success and failure principle to ensure we hit the goal.

At the end of the day, we determined what we needed was something we called a Slack Adjuster.

In the context of our situation, we needed to make up the slack in our revenue as we transitioned to a model that would bring in good revenue as we wound down the bad revenue.

The solution we came up with was a high-ticket, four-day boot camp with a price of $12,500 per attendee. We created the product with the goal of it having little to no tail. What that means is there was a defined time frame that we are willing to invest in delivery of service on this product in exchange for the money our customers invested to receive the value.

In short, we delivered the value they would get at the event, itself maximizing the revenue we generated and the return on our investment of time.

We didn't want to service clients for months or years after the initial four-day event because that would require more resources, more time, more energy, and more money. Plus, a four-day boot camp had a fixed assumption on the allocation of time and resources to fulfill the promise.

It was the perfect answer to our problem. We had the economic model built and we were at the part where all the fun began.

We needed to sell this boot camp, and we needed a marketing and sales process that would deliver high-value clients without requiring a lot of time or resources. So we had to do it right—from beginning to end. We knew the Community Funnel strategy would deliver the automated results that we were seeking, and it was time to put it to the test.

The *one thing* we needed was to deliver a clear message to the right audience in a way that would get their *attention* and then, through the consumption of our content, get them to move through the stages of the Buyer Journey: awareness, consideration, and decision.

That one thing was staring us right in the face the entire time we were doing our research.

That one thing was to write a book.

It's exactly what we did, and it was a home run.

A book allowed us to get the attention of people who did not know who we were positioned as an authority. Writing the book made getting our message consumed infinitely easier than a message that was considered "advertising."

We made over $1 million our first year using the book as the Universal Offer for the Community Funnel. The best part about it was that the entire process was completely automated and it produced solid, Market Qualified Leads (MQLs) who were ideal consumers for our boot camp.

The sale at the end of the process was simple and we built a steady pipeline of opportunities not for just boot camp sales, but also for some of the other products and services our company sold.

The Community Funnel changed our company and the way we'll do business forever. It can do the same for you and your business.

Why You Must Write a Book

We know, without a shadow of a doubt, that you need only *one* funnel to consistently get all the customers you could ever want. The good news is that anyone can implement the Community Funnel strategy if they are committed to following the principles that make a funnel successful. To create the predictability and consistency that the funnel will provide to you, you must do the following things well:

- **Create Authority** – Demonstrate to people that you are the preeminent expert in your field.
- **Attract an Audience** – Consistently capture the attention of like-minded individuals so they can learn more about you, your product or service, and your brand.
- **Increase Trust** – Build a relationship with your audience by delivering relevant, valuable content so that they get to know, like, and trust you.
- **Convert Customers** – Turn your followers into paying customers.
- **Build a Community** – Create a throng of happy and excited advocates who love you and what you do, and who want to share their passion for you with others.

The best way to do all this—to get customers consistently—is not to create a product and start promoting and selling it. Rather, it's to write a book and leverage your content to deliver value to your prospects before asking them to buy from you. As your prospects consume your content, their trust in your ability to help them increases. And, as you demonstrate that you can add value by actually helping them through your content, you become their trusted advisor—the only clear choice amongst your competitors.

You see, to this day, even with everything that is bought, sold, and delivered digitally, the number-one way to create authority is still to write and publish a book. A book is tangible evidence that you know what you're talking about. It gives you a platform to tell your stories, prove your theories, communicate your values, and inspire others. It also gives people a way to relate to you and connect with who you are, what you believe, and what you do.

Once your book is written, you'll have everything you need to make the Community Funnel strategy work for you. Your book helps you organize all your thoughts and stories and it formalizes the value you bring to your readers by putting it into a format they can consume. Simply put, your book gives you all the content you need for your funnel so you can leverage it at every step of the Buyer Journey.

Leveraged content is the strategic creation and use of content delivered through all of the different media channels that your audience pays attention to in order to increase consumption. As consumption increases, so does the trust your audience members have for you. The more trust you can build with them, the easier it is to drive them closer to becoming your customer.

Leveraged content is different from what you may know as a "money magnet" or "lead magnet," which is an ethical bribe or one piece of content that marketers offer in exchange for their prospects' contact information to get prospects into their funnel, but never use again in any other format or on any other platform. With leveraged content, you would take content from your book and leverage it across multiple media channels. For example, you can take a chapter from your book and create multiple blog posts on your website that you could then post on Facebook. You can record videos for consumption on YouTube and create podcasts with audio that you created from the material.

Your audience consumes content in different ways. With a leveraged content strategy you can deliver it up to all of the different media channels and platforms in all the formats available in order to increase consumption.

Your book will also give you content for your website. Once people go to your site and see that you've written a book, you'll have instant credibility and you'll be in a position to start building trust with a potential future customer.

The biggest benefit of writing the book isn't necessarily automating your business and making consistent, predictable income (which, by the way, we think is a very good thing); it comes from the lives you change, the connections you make, and the community that you build.

Once people read your book, they'll either be attracted to or repelled by who you are, what you say, and what you stand for. As an aside, it's okay to drive away the people who don't align with your Core Philosophy.

Your Core Philosophy is your body of knowledge on a subject matter that communicates your beliefs—beliefs that you've formed based upon everything you've learned and experienced in your life up to today. Every experience, good or bad, happy or sad, successful or not, plays a part in your Core Philosophy, which guides every decision you make about your business.

You only want to work with the people that know, like, and trust you and who are in alignment with your Core Philosophy. Your book will help you attract those people like a magnet.

Anyone Can Write a Book

At this point, you might be saying to yourself: "Wait, I just want a funnel to get customers. I'm not a writer" or "Writing a book takes too long and requires too much effort." We're here to tell you that anyone—including you—has the skills and tools available to write a meaningful, impactful book.

If you don't think you can write a book, think of it like this—imagine you bought an entertainment center from Ikea and when you opened the box, something was missing: a tool, a piece of the entertainment center, or even the instructions themselves. It would be hard—almost impossible—to assemble that piece of furniture.

Now imagine that you opened the box and the instructions were easy to read, you had access to all the tools, and none of the pieces were missing. You'd be able to assemble it in no time and even have the drawers open properly.

It's much the same way with building your funnel. You'll never build a consistent funnel, one that gets you clients today and clients tomorrow, without having all the pieces and the instructions to make it a happen. Writing your book will give you all the pieces. This book will give you the instructions to put it all together.

If you're one of the people who think that writing a book takes too long and too much effort, you must understand that the book is already inside of you. A book is simply a collection of stories that validate or demonstrate something you already know.

In his book *Tools of Titans*, Timothy Ferriss interviews people who are considered to be the Digital Presidents of their niche, people like entrepreneur and best-selling author Gary Vaynerchuk. The entire book is nothing more than people answering interview questions and sharing their thoughts and stories on specific topics.

If you can speak, you can write a book in no time. There's technology available today that can capture what you're saying as fast as you speak. There are also people out there who can ask you the right questions to extract the nuggets of gold that exist in your head. To that point, there are even ghostwriters who can take what you've dictated and turn it into an amazing book.

Roughly 80 percent of the books published today are written by someone other than the author. In the end, the content is still "authored" by the person whose name is on the front of the book, it's just that someone has to take the time to put it into a written, consumable format. We've read some amazing books that were completely inspired by nothing more than a webinar.

Think of it like using a dolly to move a huge refrigerator. Picking up the refrigerator and putting it onto a truck is infinitely easier when you have a tool like a dolly to help you get the job done. There are a number of tools you can use to get the book out of your head and onto paper without you having to pen the words or mash the keys on your computer.

Some of the best books ever written are nothing more than stories that have been captured and then written down. Additionally, some of the best books aren't that long; they can be read in an hour or two.

You have a book inside of you and it's just waiting to make its way out.

Becoming the Digital President

1. The Goal

You must start with the end in mind. For us this means you need to identify where you currently are and where you want to be. You do this by designing your "Life by Strategy." A Life by Strategy is a life lived the way you design it to be lived and funded by the work you love to do. In short, you want to make sure that your exchange of time for income are in alignment with what you love to do.

Our Core Philosophy originated from our love of helping our clients acquire customers for their business while living their Life by Strategy. At the same time, we are living ours doing meaningful work, building meaningful relationships and getting paid for not what we do, but how we think. Most importantly, we've created tremendous leverage in our business so that we have the opportunity to live the life we've designed for ourselves—on our own terms.

Doing this means we create value for others while our toes are in the sand, next to our wives and children. Being able to do all of these things on a daily basis are our true loves (and they provide generously for our families and lifestyles at the same time) without us having to make sacrifices on our purpose in life.

In his book, *4-Hour Workweek*, Tim Ferriss talks about how you can create the life of your dreams if you shift your thinking about money, time, and family. He maintains that we need to think not about making millions and billions of dollars, but rather about how we can enjoy the lifestyle we want and spend more time with our family by focusing more on what we love to do and working smarter while we do it.

Ferriss sums up this philosophy in this quote from the book: "The question you should be asking isn't, 'What do I want?' or 'What are my goals?' but 'What would excite me?'"

2. Hit Maker

A Hit Maker is someone who provides a highly differentiated product or service that adds significant value in solving the problems and challenges of their Ideal Client. The goal of a Hit Maker is to remove constraints, provide a framework for success, alter thought processes, collapse time, and provide leverage to the people in their marketplace.

In doing this, the Hit Maker earns a tremendous amount of authority within the market and has the ability to influence people and the decisions they make about them, the Hit Maker themselves, and using their product or service.

Your goal is to create a hit product and then write a book that tells consumers in your industry how you (and it) can make their pain go away faster and easier than anyone else—including themselves.

The dating app Tinder was created by some guys who were buddies at USC in 2012. They created it as a way for people to use a social media site to meet strangers rather than connecting with people with whom they were already familiar, something most other sites couldn't or wouldn't do. By May of 2013, Tinder had become one of the top 25 social networking apps available on the internet based upon number of people who used it and how often it was utilized.

By the end of 2013, a little over a year later, Tinder became one of the only online dating services to be recognized as one of the top five most-used internet services in the prior decade.

Tinder was a hit product that took off and changed the way people met each other online and on mobile devices.

3. Audience

As we mentioned earlier, you're not looking to attract everyone to you so you can work with them. You're actually looking to work only with people who are in alignment with your Core Philosophy and who see value in the solutions to provide to their problem.

To boil it down even further, you're really only looking to speak to one person. We call this the Only One Principle.

Through the Only One Principle, you will speak to someone who fits your definition of an Ideal Client Profile (ICP). Your ICP is the person whose pains and gains your solution addresses very specifically. Your ICP is the person to whom your promise of success rings true when they decide to work with you. Your ICP is someone who is attracted to you, what you have to say, and what you stand for. When you talk to only one person, you will repel anyone who is not your ICP.

Your goal is to start with identifying and then building your audience. Once you decide who your ICP is, you can then introduce your product. It's audience first, product second.

In 2008, Jimmy Iovine and Dr. Dre partnered to bring Beats headphones to the market. Iovine had significant influence and credibility in the music space and Dr. Dre had a significant following of athletes, musicians, and other influencers inside and outside of the music industry.

Together, they built a decidedly niche audience by leveraging relationships with other influencers. Then, they all worked together to build a global audience by creating a massive awareness campaign around a new brand that was positioned differently than just an ordinary set of headphones. Today Beats owns a 40 percent market share of the headphone industry.

4. Core Content

As your Universal Offer, your book is going to be where your audience first learns of how you can solve their problems and achieve their desires. By defining and refining your Core Philosophy and distilling it down to the real value you bring to the table, you'll be able to write a solid book that delivers the Core Content your target market and buyer personas will absolutely want to read.

By aligning all of your Core Stories in the book to your Core Philosophy, you create the Core Content that will create awareness in your target market to attract and build an audience of people that look to you as an authority around helping them go from where they are to where they want to be.

Your Core Philosophy and all the Core Stories that support it create a Core Messaging strategy that will be pervasive in everything you do: your book cover, the book title, the book subtitle, your website, and in all the content you distribute.

Aligning your Core Philosophy with your Core Stories to create a Core Message also helps you attract, educate, entertain and build a relationship with your audience so you can continue to influence them to become a client and then a raving fan. It also makes it clear to them what you can do to help them with their problems.

When Steve Jobs came back to Apple in the mid-'90s, he completely changed the strategy of how Apple was going to approach its client base. Jobs felt that rather than trying to be everything to everyone, Apple needed to focus their Core Message on a specific group of consumers and solve their problems at a high level. To do this, he slashed its number of technology offerings from 20-plus to just four amazing products: a consumer desktop, a consumer notebook, a pro desktop, and a pro notebook.

However, most people don't understand the true brilliance in Steve Jobs. Jobs understood that nobody really cared about the specific "boxes" they made, rather, they cared about what Apple stood for. Knowing this, he wanted to take lessons he learned from other great companies like Nike to build and strengthen the Apple brand.

Jobs knew Nike's success wasn't due to the fact that they advertised sneakers and apparel. It was a result of their continued efforts to, as Jobs put it, to: "honor great athletes and great athletics." All of Nike's content aligned to that message and their status as a perennial athletics apparel company is proof of that.

With that fundamental understanding, Jobs realized Apple had to get clear on their Core Content as it related to their Core Values and Core Message: people with passion can change the world for better. It was already inside them as a company, Job's challenge was to communicated it to the world.

The message he came up with at the time was: "Think Different" with a tagline of "People who are crazy enough to think they can change the world actually do."

Twenty years later, that is still the company's credo and Apple went from near bankruptcy to the most highly valued company on the planet. We think he got his message right.

5. The Book

Once you've designed your Life by Strategy, identified who your ICP is, and aligned your Core Philosophies with your Core Stories, it's time to write your book.

Your book gives you the content to create an inbound marketing strategy—with a strong Universal Offer—to organize all of your thoughts, stories, and ideas and create a linear path for your client to take so they can get from where they are to where they want to be. The book will address all of their issues, challenges, and situations by giving them solid, real-world solutions they can use.

Most importantly, your book will make you the go-to expert in your niche. When that happens, all the fun begins.

In 2004, Gary Keller, founder of Keller Williams Real Estate, wrote *The Millionaire Real Estate Agent* with Dave Jenks and Jay Papasan. At the time, Keller Williams was the sixth-largest real estate agency in the United States.

Gary's business model was all about recruiting agents. He has a simple philosophy: Everyone needs to follow the influencers. Leveraging a model that allowed people to recruit agents and build passive revenue, Gary provided his army of recruiters with a very strong "Universal Offer" that allowed anyone to clearly deliver a message that would make them aware of the new model and its value propositions.

Since the writing of that book, Keller Williams has exploded and now sits at the top of the list as the largest real estate company by agent count in the world.

Keller, Jenks, and Papasan (as well as just Keller and Papasan) have written several books since, and all of them are best sellers.

6. Content Hub

Your goal at this point is to start getting subscribers with whom you can continue to build a relationship and eventually convert to paying customers. You will use content from your book—even if it hasn't been published—to populate the various platforms available to you for content dissemination.

In order to get subscribers, you'll want to make sure that your Content Hub is up and running. Your Content Hub is your website. It's a great way to leverage some of your brand story messaging. It is also where all of your key content is housed for people to come, make an initial consumption of your content, get access to your book which is "Coming Soon," and to sign up for future communication from—and content releases by—you.

Your Content Hub is a key distribution channel for you and is essentially the subscriber mechanism you'll use to attract people who want to find more out about you and what you do. It's where the main call to action will be for your book as well.

Most people have a Content Hub sitting under their nose and they use it every day: their Facebook page. There are millions of personal, business, and community pages in existence today, and they all produce a variety of content from articles to videos and everything in between.

Facebook has given every person on the planet their own Content Hub because it leverages the fundamental principle of sharing with an audience. It's something most of us do naturally every day and it's a hugely powerful concept in building and strengthening a community. Consider how long Facebook would remain in existence if everyone stopped sharing content all at once. Likely, it wouldn't take long.

7. Community Funnel Canvas

To ensure that your Community Funnel produces consistent opportunities for you, you'll need to map out your ICP's journey from not knowing you to becoming a subscriber, from a subscriber to a lead, from an lead to a client, from a client to a promoter, and from a promoter to an advocate in the community you'll need in order to grow your business deep and wide.

Your Community Funnel canvas will include a schematic of the journey your customer will take along that path from unknown to advocate. You can get a look at it in Figure 1 below. The construction of your canvas will start with your book and then include elements like keyword research, calls to action, your website, as well as content distribution like blogs, podcasts, videos, social media, etc.

And, to ensure that your content will be consumed in a variety of formats by your target audience, you'll also need to create a Leveraged Consumption Matrix with the placement strategy for your content. You'll need to know what type of content you will deliver, in what media you will deliver it, in what context it will be delivered, when you will deliver it, as well as the overall goal you're looking to accomplish.

Figure 1

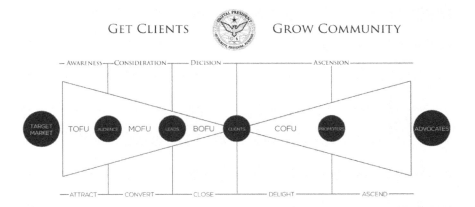

8. Community

One of the most important parts of becoming Digital President is creating a huge community of followers who share the same values and philosophies as you. It also allows you to leverage two of the most powerful basic human needs: love and belonging. To create a strong community, you must understand and employ the principles of engagement and promotion.

At the outset of building your community, you must engage with the members of your community and have them engage back with you. They're in your community because they like you and want to learn from you. You must give them access to what they're here for: you.

You'll engage with them using content, asking questions, running Q&As, and doing other things that give you a presence in your community. The great news is that once you get the engagement process going, your community members will start engaging with each other (which requires less interaction from you).

Through the construction of your community and regular engagement, promoters and advocates will spring up from within the group. These people will be the ones who keep the engagement going in the community and reach outside of the community to bring new people into the fold. They will also do things to bring you over to their platform(s) and introduce you to the people they know to help you build your community.

At some point, you'll likely not need to do a whole lot to keep your community active and excited about you and your business.

It's much like CrossFit is today. There are over 7,000 CrossFit-affiliated gyms worldwide with approximately $2 billion in net revenues. It's a huge enterprise, but the chance that a CrossFit gym will close and go out of business is only 2 percent.

There's not just one CrossFit exercise program, company figurehead, or gym style across the globe, yet the camaraderie, values, and variety shared by the members of the CrossFit community keep it strong, profitable, and successful.

Who Will Want to Read This Book?

Without a doubt, there are strategies we share in this book that could and would be helpful to many business owners in improving and growing their enterprise. In fact, many of the principles we cover would apply to business owners who are at just about every stage of growing their business.

In the end, though, we realize that we can't be all things to all people and that this book wouldn't be helpful (or fun to read) if we tried to solve every business owner's problems. Subsequently, we decided to focus the message of this book for these distinct categories of business owners:

Entrepreneurs: Consistent, Predictable Customer Acquisition will transform your business and your life. More importantly you'll never have to worry about where you're next client is coming from again.

Marketers: Experience the difference between advertising and leveraged content marketing so you can have an unlimited budget to acquire customers.

Coaches and Consultants: When you're positioned as a high-level authority, you'll be able to increase your sales and your prices. More importantly you'll have the leverage you need to only do the things you want to do.

Authors: Turn your book into a highly leveraged, profitable business.

Professional Service Providers: Clarify your message and establish yourself as an authority so you can attract an audience and get clients fast without having to be salesy.

This book is also for anybody who wants to:

- Attract an audience of your ideal clients that pay attention to you
- Instantly be positioned as an authority in your niche
- Create high value offers that convert
- Publish content that is so good your subscribers would actually pay for it
- Speed up the sales process through leveraged consumption
- Maximize customer value through the Value Exchange
- Build a Funnel to convert clients through automation
- Build a community of loyal followers and brand advocates

Having lost $8 billion in 1993, IBM, which had weathered the onslaught of technological change—from punch cards to supercomputers—faced a terrible conclusion: innovate or go out of business.

IBM chose the former. They moved away from the hardware game—constructing and marketing low-margin personal computers, fabricating computer chips and printers, and building and selling other hardware. Instead, they decided to focus on providing IT expertise and business services to other businesses.

The decision was a huge success. By 2010, Big Blue—one of the original Digital Presidents—had acquired over 200 companies from the IT services sector and put itself on track to be the number-one purveyor of enterprise server solutions in the world by 2013.

Becoming the Digital President of your niche is possible no matter how big or small your company is and no matter how bad things may have gotten. The experiences and insights we share in *Digital President* are from our own successes and failures. They are the lessons we learned both as a startup company and as a company that stalled and came back with a fury to create consistent, predictable income for ourselves, our families, and the people we work with every day.

More importantly, we found a way to create a Life by Strategy that allows us to add tremendous value to other people's lives while we live the life we've always dreamed of.

Digital President will show you, step by step, what we did to create the only funnel you will ever need—the Community Funnel, write a book to make that funnel run like a well-oiled machine, and build a thriving community that will serve you and your company for years and years to come.

Your Map for This Book

Sir Isaac Newton once said: "Truth is ever to be found in simplicity, and not in the multiplicity and confusion of things."

Our goal in writing *Digital President* was to give you a clear understanding of the path you'll need to take between where you are now and where you want to be as Digital President of your space.

To that end, we've laid everything out in sequential order, chapter by chapter. What this means is that you'll want and need to do the things we're instructing you to do in the order we tell you to do them to get the most from the book. In addition, you're going to want to follow the steps as we've laid them out to get the most from your funnel and leveraged content strategy.

We've layered in several stories, anecdotes, and real-life experiences to help you relate your current situation to similar challenges we faced in the past and how we addressed and overcame them. Our belief is that you will be inspired and excited to do the same in your business using the strategies that we used.

Some of the chapters have a lot of information so you can get your head around the principles we are trying to teach you. They are going to be longer than some of the other chapters, but they will still be chock-full of valuable information and strategies.

Our goal is to teach and entertain you while you internalize what you need to in order to become the Digital President of the space where you are the go-to expert on what you do. We promise that if you follow our instructions and do things the way we suggest that you do them, you'll have an automated business and the only funnel you'll ever need to create the life that you've always wanted for yourself.

Three important steps to help you get the most value from this book:

Step 1: Join the Life By Strategy community on Facebook. If you want to live your Life By Strategy, get valuable content and join a network of like-minded high achievers that are committed to financial and time freedom, go to **digitalpresident.com/community**.

Step 2: Access the free resources. Throughout the book we'll reference helpful resources that you can access for free at **digitalpresident.com/resources**.

Step 3: Give feedback and get help. We read every email. We love to hear your feedback and help you if you're stuck. E-mail us **feedback@digitalpresident.com**.

CHAPTER 1

LIVING A LIFE BY STRATEGY

———

"A life best lived is a life by design. Not by accident, and not by just walking through the day careening from wall to wall and managing to survive. That's okay. But if you can start giving your life dimensions and design and color and objectives and purpose, the results can be staggering."

—Jim Rohn

We were recently approached with the opportunity to buy an extremely profitable nutritional supplement business. The company was tracking for a run rate of just under $1 million in sales in its first eight months in business and had consistently grown over the course of a year. The owner, a 28-year-old fitness celebrity and entrepreneur, was willing to sell at a significant discount so he could focus on another business in which he was making over $1 million per week.

At face value the deal looked really good. Maybe a little too good. As we went through the process we use to evaluate opportunities, we uncovered some challenges that impacted the most critical factor in our decision making process:

Return On Time (ROT)

We were originally considering this deal based on the fact the business was currently successful with many Stock Keeping Units (SKU) and the brand had been built online with solid celebrity endorsements. We could turn this business into an online hit, the question was: "At what sacrifice?"

What appeared to be a for-sure deal from everyone's point of view, was unsettled for us. The part that was in question was the time commitment on our part to make the opportunity successful.

At the end of the day, however, it aligned with our Life by Strategy as it pertained to time. There was a skill that we specifically wanted to acquire—how to be successful with e-commerce—so we could leverage our core talents of marketing and getting clients.

The business offered us a way to build passive income while aligning to the areas we wanted to grow. It also gave us the chance to spend time with the right people and because of that, we were willing to make the investment.

The sacrifice and exchange of time was well worth the investment, and If you would have told us 10 years earlier when we got started online that a seven-figure income opportunity would be boiled down the amount of time it would take to make that income truly passive, we never would've believed you.

However, that is exactly what was happening. When you can invest one dollar and get back ten dollars while you sleep, why would you ever go trade that time for money, especially when you could be spending your time doing things that are truly priceless like snowboarding in Aspen, Colorado or searching for sand dollars in Naples, Florida?

The truth is you're either *leveraging* your time, or you're *trading* it. We both made the decision a long time ago to no longer trade our time for money and only leverage our time to get the maximum ROI.

Understanding a Life by Strategy

You are the strategist for your life.

You are in charge of your plan and of how you use your resources of time, energy, and money. As a result of this level of control, you, as a strategist, will always have a move you can make to get closer to the outcome you seek.

More importantly, as a strategist, you will always be in position to win.

Your job as a strategist is to create a strategy to achieve a goal.

A strategy is just another word for a plan. When you create a strategy, you're devising a plan of how you're going to achieve a specific outcome.

It's important to note here that strategy is *not* the actions you take to make the plan a reality.

Those actions are called tactics.

Tactics are the actual means used to reach an objective.

Once your strategy is in place, you are going to employ specific and measured tactics to achieve your goal.

Here's how strategy applies to us in our lives: If we're working *in* our business and living our daily lives, then we are only being tactical in nature. We take action every day and we get results—expected or unexpected.

Once we step out of our daily life and start planning what we want to be, do, and have, we're now working on our life and implementing a strategy.

We always need to start planning around a "why" and getting clear on:
- Why we want to end up with one outcome instead of another
- Why we are choosing one thing over another
- Why we would say yes to one thing versus saying no to something else

It's about having a clear filter for your life goals.

Every day you are either moving closer to or further away from your goals. Designing a Life by Strategy gives you the clarity on things you need to start and stop doing to make it a reality.

If what you are doing in your life and business are not yielding the results you want, it's likely because you don't have a good strategy in place. Moreover, it's possible that you don't have a plan to get you from where you are to where you want to be.

The good news is you choose what to do, how you do it, and with whom you do it.

The exciting thing is this: As soon as you get really clear on your passion and purpose and what gives you the most fulfillment, you'll be able to design a plan for how you can exchange both your time and money to create tremendous value in the marketplace.

And once that happens, you can accomplish *all* your goals, especially as they relate to how you're going to invest your time in the right strategy for you so you can reap the maximum return on your investment of time.

To help you with designing a Life by Strategy, let's first take a closer look at what it is.

1. Owning your time

A Life by Strategy is about time.

Motivational speaker and personal development expert Jim Rohn had some strong beliefs about time and how valuable it is to all of us. We love what he says about time here: "Time is more value than money. You can get more money, but you cannot get more time."

If you've never thought about time that way, then it's time you do.

Have you ever sat down and thought about how valuable your time really is?

We're not asking if you know your hourly worth. We want to know if you've ever thought long and hard about the true value of your time—of anybody's time, for that matter.

If you haven't, that's okay, because you're going to do that in designing your Life by Strategy.

If you have, then what we're about to share will reinforce any conclusions you've come to about how valuable it really is.

Check this out:

Imagine there is a bank that every morning deposits $86,400 into your account.

And every day it happens over and over again. The only catch, according to this idea, is that you cannot save that particular deposit until the next day.

The $86,400 you get in the morning is gone in the evening. You can't use any of it in advance and you can't pile it up.

What would you do?

Would you think carefully about how you'd use it every day?

Would you make sure that the account was completely empty at the end of each day?

The thing is, we all have this account available to us—except it's time we get to use. We all have 86,400 seconds to spend every day, and at the end of the day, they're gone.

Does the thought of the seconds slipping away stress you out?

Can you hear the tick, tick, tick of the clock?

Well, the seconds will continue to blip away.

You can't keep them or bank them, but you can use them wisely.

And by "wisely," we're not talking just about producing stuff.

We're speaking specifically about how you use this account with the limited time deposit each day—how you invest your time shrewdly so that you get the best possible return in terms of health, happiness, and success.

In order to get the best return on where you invest your time, you must put a plan together of how, when, and where you're going to spend it.

You start with asking yourself some really simple questions.

- What is your *goal?*
- Where are you trying to go?
- Why is that the *goal?*
- Is that really the *goal?*

You want to be absolutely crystal clear on the goal you have for your life.

- Where do you want to spend your time?
- Where do you want to spend your money?

Every day you are either moving closer to your goal or further away, and like with any goal, there are many different ways to accomplish it.

As well, there is a good strategy and a bad strategy to get you to the outcome you seek.

A good strategy is solving the right problem. A bad strategy is solving the wrong problem.

It's important to keep this in mind when determining how and where you're going to spend your time.

In a Life by Strategy, your goal is to spend your time doing the things you love—that don't feel like work.

A good strategy will allow you to do just that.

When you live a Life by Strategy, you're living your life without sacrificing the congruency of money, time, and the things from which you get the most fulfillment when you invest your time and money.

2. Getting clear

A Life by Strategy is the process of becoming crystal clear on what makes up the gap between where you are and where you want to be.

Closing that gap means something different to everyone; however, the process to close that gap is still the same for each and every one of us.

Getting clear on how you accomplish your goals in closing that gap while staying congruent to your personal Core Values is the "Core Promise" philosophy.

Your Core Promise is at the foundation of living a Life by Strategy.

It's a promise you make to your Ideal Client, yourself, and to the market.

It's a promise to your Ideal Client that you can actually deliver to them the specific outcomes they desire in working with you.

At the same time, you're making a promise to yourself that through delivering to your clients what they want, you will move yourself closer to your goals and desired outcomes.

You're also making a pledge to the market that you would never compromise the value you create, deliver, and promise in exchange for money.

Like all promises, these are a declaration that you will do a particular thing.

The important thing to note here is that a "Core Promise" is not simply measured by money. It's also measured by the congruence of doing what you love, while creating massive value, which allows you to do more of what you love (and get paid to do in the end).

Discovering Your Core Promise

The process of determining your Core Promise starts with a real simple exercise.

Step 1 – Brainstorm all the things you would love to be, do, or have if money were no object.

Be creative with this part of the process and put on some music that gets your creative juices flowing.

If you want, pretend it's Christmas and put on some Christmas music to get you in the mood of thinking about what you'd really like to enjoy in life if there were no limits of time and money.

Remember, the only limits on this list are the ones you put on it.

Once you've created your list, arrange those items into columns marked daily, weekly, quarterly, annually, and every 10 years.

The cool thing about this exercise is you don't have to ever have done any of these things before.

Remember, this list includes ***everything*** you love or think you would love.

Let me give you an example from my list.

I've never had a full-time chef. But, I do love to eat.
What I love even more is when someone creates a well-thought-out meal for me.

In fact, I'd love to have someone prepare my meals for me every day.

This one is high on my list.

So, if you would love to go on a walk with you wife and kids each day, put the amount of time you'd like to allocate to that. If you want to read to your kids, put down how long you would want to do that. If you would love to meditate or read, you're going to want an estimate for how long that would take.

While you're doing this exercise, think in a linear time frame from the time you wake up until the time you go to bed.

- What time would you wake up?
- Where would you be?
- What would you eat?
- Would you read a book?
- Would you be writing a book?
- Which book, or what subject?

Again, the goal is to get a really clear picture of what you ***love*** to do.

Once you're done creating the list, categorize each entry as "providing total fulfillment" to "it would be nice to have."

Step 2 – Take everything you've identified as daily and write down how much time— exactly—you would spend doing each activity yourself.

Each activity should have a cost of time and/or money associated with it.

You're looking to see how much you're going to need of each resource.

The goal here is to end up with a dollar amount that you'll need to free up for yourself so you can spend your time doing the things that bring you the most fulfillment.

The amount you need is your *Freedom Number*. Your Freedom Number is the recurring income you need monthly to "buy your time back" so you're free to do what you love each day.

Write down your Freedom Number. Make sure you have that number front and center every day.

Step 3 – Drill down the "who."

Now that you've listed out all of the things you love to do, make a list of all the people you would want to spend time with doing these things you love.

For example, Michael loves to snowboard and he also enjoys relaxing at the lake. He doesn't love each of these activities equally. At the same time, he doesn't enjoy doing those things with the same people.

Consequently, he has to specifically break out his activities so that he matches what he loves doing with the people with whom he enjoys doing those things.

Also, you may have children like we do. And, if your children are anything like ours, they may not share your definition of fun. As such, you'll need to take that into consideration as you're working through this process.

Creating a list and then figuring out what we would do with whom was extremely hard for us. So, we asked an additional question to add some emotion to the process: "What would we do with the people we loved the most if we only had one last day to spend with them?"

Taking this additional approach helped us (and it will help you) really focus in on who and what matter most.

Step 4 – Filter out what you don't want to do.

Once you've completed the first three steps, the next filter you need to add in order to give context to your list is add all the things you now do—personally and professionally—that *you don't enjoy.*

It could be something as simple as not being able to be home when your kids are home.

It doesn't matter. If you don't like it, put it on the list.

For us it's really simple: We do not like to do things we do not want to do.

There is nothing more draining and unfulfilling than doing something you just don't like or want to do. You may even find that true in your own current business.

If you're like we are, however, you'll do the things you don't like to do—don't want to do—because you love to bring value to people.

You want to get clear on what you don't want to do because in living a Life by Strategy 1) you're looking to never do those things again, and 2) you want to focus on what gives you the most fulfillment.

Step 5 – Align your Core Promise with the core problems in your marketplace.

At this point, you really need to think hard about how your Core Promise is going to add enough value to the people in your marketplace so you can solve their core problem.

Remember, you're not just looking to exchange your time and product for money.

That's what you do now.

You're looking to solve the core problems in your niche or industry in such a way that you live a vibrant, exciting, and fulfilled life all while you're adding a tremendous amount of value in solving them.

Here are some questions you can ask yourself to get clear on how and what would provide the most value to solving the problem and still give you a tremendous amount of fulfillment at the same time:

Let's say a good friend of yours had a problem in their business that they just couldn't solve. And the only days you could help your friend would be the days you take off from work. What would need to be at the core of their problem in order for you to be willing to help them with your personal time? More specifically, what value would they need you to bring to them that would still give you the most fulfillment out of helping them?

A core problem could be that they need to design a brand. It could be they are trying to get more people to visit their yoga studio. For that matter, it could be that they are trying to find more investors to purchase investment properties. It could be they are trying to purchase investment properties themselves.

It can be any problem at all.

We both have extensive experience in the real estate industry—across a number of verticals—and as such, we are more than qualified to help someone find and purchase a home. As well, we are highly qualified to help someone invest in real estate.

All of that said, we don't get any fulfillment from delivering the solutions geared towards purchasing and investing in a home.

What we do get a tremendous amount of fulfillment from is laying out a strategy that would allow someone to leverage predictive data and marketing to build a funnel to deliver more qualified opportunities to real estate agents who are trying to build their business.

As you can see, the marketplace is the same in both examples: real estate.

The difference is that the core problem we like to solve is also in alignment with what gives us the most fulfillment.

There is nothing we *love* to work on more than helping someone with a core problem find customers and build a system and process for predictable customer acquisition.

Have you figured it out yet?

Do you know the core problem that you can solve in your arena?

Don't worry if you haven't … you'll figure it out.

The goal is to drill down to the core problem.

If you think of your Core Promise as the solution to the core problem; you'll find that your answer rests right there.

Please don't shortcut this process.

The difference in living a life by a good strategy versus living a life by a bad strategy hinges on you nailing your core problem and Core Promise.

Putting Your Core Promise to Work

Once you have your Core Promise dialed in, you'll want to create a list of all the ways you can provide value with it.

After you've completed your list, identify what you think the Value Exchange rate is for each strategy and prioritize them from high value to low value.

Your promise can't be something that's nice to have.

It needs to be something that is a *must* have.

To arrive at a solid list of high-value strategies you can provide, you can ask yourself the following questions:

- What are all the ways I can create value for this client?

- How does the client measure that value?
- What are they willing to exchange for the value I provide?
- What would the average person pay to instantly receive the results given by your Core Promise?

Here's a real-world example based upon our strategy to deliver extremely high value in solving a problem: finding customers and building a system and process for predictable customer acquisition for a real estate investor.

We could do any and all of the following:

- Go out and look for homes that were in pre-foreclosure and find the investor a potential property to buy as an investment.
- Provide them with a list of addresses for homeowners that have filed for a divorce and/or missed credit card payments.
- Provide them with the phone numbers and direct mail strategies to contact prospects.
- Provide them a PDF swipe file of a successful postcard or even let them use my vendor for creating the card and then mailing it.
- Manage the entire lead generation process and even field calls from our marketing efforts, and provide them with qualified investment opportunities.
- We could even write a book on how to go from where my Ideal Client is to where they want to go (no matter where they are now).

Those are all viable Core Promises that provide a significant amount of value in solving the core problem of real estate investors.

That said, each solution is a different model.

And each model comes with a different set of challenges, obstacles, bottlenecks, and constraints.

No matter what model you choose, you're looking for your Ideal Client to identify with your Core Promise and then be willing and wanting to pay you to let you help solve their problem.

What you'll find when you apply this principle to your business is the less time it takes for your Ideal Client to experience the value you provide, the more money they are willing to exchange for it.

At the end of this process, you really should be very clear on what type of clients you want and what the promise is that you're going to fulfill in order to capture the value you create in the marketplace.

You are now headed to what we like to call The Promised Land, where the life you so richly deserve is ready to be created by you.

It's Time to Live a Life by Strategy

Living a Life by Strategy means that you subscribe to the belief that we live in a created world.

In a created world you can do anything you want.

A created world is the opposite of a reported world.

In a reported world, people tell you that you can't reach your dreams, that you can't create a multi-million dollar business and be fulfilled by what you do every day.

In a reported world, there are lies and limiting beliefs holding people back from living the life—and having the business—of their dreams.

A person in a reported world says, "I can't do that because I don't have enough time, money, or skill."

If you ever thought you could not do something because of those reasons, it's time for you to stop living in a reported world and start living in a created world.

Here's a new framework for how to think when living in a created world:

- In a created world there is always a way—you just might not know it yet.
- In a created world you ask yourself: "If I had to, how would I?"
- In a created world you acknowledge that *life* can be *whatever you want it to be.*

Right now, the only constraint, obstacle, or bottleneck holding you back from living a Life by Strategy is your thinking.

That's it.

Take the time right now to follow the steps we outlined in this chapter:

- Make the decision that you want it better than you have today—better for you, your family, your clients, and your industry.
- Believe that time is your most precious commodity and make the decision that you want your time to be spent doing something that's fulfilling each and every day.
- Get clear on what it is you love to do.
- Get even clearer on who is going to be taking this journey with you.
- Figure out what your Core Promise is.
- Determine what your Ideal Client's core problem is.
- Identify how your Core Promise is going to add a tremendous amount of value to help solve your client's problem so that they would be willing to pay anything to have you do so.

- Make sure that when you do this every day, it's the most rewarding thing you've ever done.
- Live in a created world and love what you do every day.

Too many people measure how successful they are by how much money they make or the people that they associate with. In our opinion, true success should be measured by how happy you are.

It's time to live a Life by Strategy where you get to do what you love every day.

Check out the process we use to get super clear on our goals and how to achieve them at digitalpresident.com/resources under **Deconstruct Any Goal In Any Area Of Your Life**

CHAPTER 2

THE HITMAKER

———

"Don't find customers for your products, find products for your customers."

—Seth Godin

In 2011, professional snowboarder Travis Rice and movie producer Curtis Morgan changed the way that the world looked at snowboarding forever with their release of the film *The Art of Flight*.

Having worked on another project together before, they knew what it took to create—as they put it—"a movie that was a game changer." For them, the movie had to be different from all the other skiing and snowboarding movies ever produced— including the film they made with sunglass giant Oakley a few years before.

The cinematography was cutting edge. The angles and shots of the snowboarders were the most unique and breathtaking that have ever been in a movie of this type. The jumps were electrifying and the drops from helicopters, mountain tops, and ski lifts were higher and more dangerous than they had ever been. The music was incredible and the sound was mixed at the world-famous Skywalker Ranch for which Dolby had just developed and installed brand-new audio servers.

Canada's leader in action sports, *SBC Business*, described the movie as: "Equal parts stunning action and harrowing adventure mixed with the inevitable drama."

To further accomplish their goal, rather than produce a film with characters in specific roles and specific scenes, Rice and Morgan shot the movie in breathtaking locales and filmed participants accomplishing some of the most exciting and amazing freestyle snowboarding ever recorded … as it happened.

Red Bull, which helped finance and produce the movie, acknowledged that *The Art of Flight* ranks as one of the biggest and most successful ventures in which they have participated on a global basis. Next to the Olympics, nothing has made snowboarding more present with a mainstream audience than has *The Art of Flight*. More importantly, nothing has brought to light what it means to be a professional snowboarder with such accuracy and realism in today's day and age as the movie itself.

In the end, to an external audience, *The Art of Flight* is a film that transcends snowboarding and appeals to anyone who has an appreciation for exploration, excitement, and the evolution of things.

Proof of how much the movie transcended its target audience of snowboarders comes in the form of a quote from Rice shortly after the movie's release: "People are losing their minds, and coming up to me with tears in their eyes … everyone from men in business suits, to older ladies, to the kids, they're all coming to the film. That's what is unique about this film, it speaks to a very wide audience."

Further proof of the movie's power and its ability to speak to an even broader audience was its success online, in retail stores, and at the movie theater.

For instance, the trailer of one of Rice's prior movies, *That's it, That's All*, received 500,000 views during its first three years online. When the trailer for *The Art of Flight* was released, it received more than a half million views … within the first 72 hours. Within four months, it was seen by more than seven million people.

It was marketed for sale in 750 Best Buy stores for Christmas that year and it sold out in virtually every movie theater in America for an average of $20 per person (even though the HD version was available for download at $9.99 on iTunes).

At the end of the day, the movie was a hit in every sense of the word and Travis Rice and Curtis Morgan are undoubtedly the Digital Presidents of the snowboarding world.

What It Takes to Be a Hit Maker

You might think that you need to start with an amazing product that makes a ton of money in order to be a Hit Maker. The fact of the matter is that's not necessarily the case.

A Hit Maker doesn't just deliver a hit, it's a hit with a clearly differentiated message. If you're going to be a Hit Maker, you have to solve a real problem. Moreover, you need to do it in such a way that once you solve that problem, life's going to be infinitely easier for that person from the second the problem is solved.

And it all starts with the right mindset and focus.

According to *Forbes* magazine, eight out of 10 businesses fail because business owners focus more on bringing dollars through the door and making money more than they do on providing a product or service that delivers a tremendous amount of value to consumers by solving their biggest problems.

The truth is, you could easily have a hit product by identifying the toughest obstacles that the consumers in your marketplace face and then be obsessed with delivering solutions that help them overcome those obstacles faster and easier than anyone else—including the customer themself—could ever do.

Your goal in developing a hit product is to remove constraints, provide a framework for success, alter thought processes, collapse time, and provide leverage to the people in your marketplace.

To accomplish this, your mindset has to be centered around understanding your customer's entire journey: the Value Journey. You do that by looking at things through that person's eyes using what we call the Only One Principle.

More specifically, you look at your strategy, messaging, and communication at every stage of the process from only one person's perspective: that of your Ideal Client.

You'll learn more about the Only One Principle and the Value Journey in Chapters 3 and 4, respectively.

As part of the process, you'll have to ask yourself questions like:

- Where are my prospects currently and where do they want to go?
- What are all the milestones and stages that they would go through in order to get there?
- When I was in their shoes, what do I wish someone would have told me?

Only when you have the answers to questions like these, can you intelligently dissect the process and give them the direction they truly need. It's like holding their hand and taking them down the path yourself to help them get there.

The trick in making a hit is to help them solve their problems and add tremendous value without asking them for a dollar before you start to help them. It's almost as if you're treating the process like you're mentoring someone who wants to learn from you. You give them the road map, the templates, the words, the activities, the schedule you use—you give them everything they need to be successful. At that point, they will be supremely grateful for all that you've done and be ready to consume your product or service.

As Digital President, writing a book is the number-one way to communicate your value. A book is like a long-form sales letter and it allows you to scale your communication of value. You can't scale the value you bring to the table any easier than you can with a book. It allows you to communicate your value to your consumer in your own words. If it's really going to create value for them, there's no better way to make it happen than to write a book and outline specifically what they need to know to solve their problem.

Write the book that you wish someone would have written for you and distill down what value is to you and what value you can bring to the marketplace. That's the surest way to not only deliver value, but also to make sure your product or service is a true hit.

In addition to creating a hit and writing a book, you need to do more than be part of the production of that hit or the author of that book—you also need to create a community. A community is a loyal group of followers who are aligned with you and what you do, and who are excited to tell others about how you can help them solve their problems and make their businesses and lives better.

To help build your community, create a shirt for members to latch onto and to show their pride of membership and affiliation with you. Connect and relate to the members of your community and have them relate to you through language that is specific to you and what you do. Connect and relate to them through the methodology you constructed to communicate and provide value to them. Doing all of these things allows people who are already like you and in alignment with you to connect with you at a higher level and vice versa.

You can leverage your authority as an author to build your community. Your authority will help you get people to follow and connect with you so much so that they may even connect with each other at a high level because they share an affinity for you and ultimately with each other. They will tell people what your solution is and why your solution is the best. They can also go to the internet and find a tremendous amount of information, support, testimonials, etc., about your product and service.

Something worth mention here is that a Hit Maker is not a one-hit wonder. One-hit wonders are what we call "carnival marketers." Carnival marketers distribute something of low value in exchange for a buck. They're not looking to add a lot of value and change lives; they're looking to make money.

A Hit Maker is the Digital President in their marketplace whose success has been so great in delivering value that they've already delivered hits and it's expected that everything they're going to continue to deliver will be a hit too.

In the end, you can be a Hit Maker if you can tell stories, because if you can tell stories, you can teach. If you can teach, you can write a book. If you can write a book, you can win the crowd. And if you can win the crowd, you can win your freedom.

As long as you can do these things—and be entertaining along the way—you can position yourself as the only solution in your marketplace and be the go-to expert from whom everyone wants to learn and with whom everyone wants to associate.

When you do, you, too, will have a hit in every sense of the word, and undoubtedly will become the Digital President of your niche.

The Benefits of Being a Hit Maker

Being a Hit Maker will change your life, and the lives of those who associate with you, forever. Here are five major benefits that you and your business will experience when you bring a hit product to the market:

Benefit #1 – Authority, Influence, and Preeminence in Your Marketplace

A Hit Maker has a preeminence mindset as *they* are the preeminent choice in their marketplace. Preeminence means that you surpass all others at what you do.

As a Hit Maker, you use a specific method to garner preeminence as well as overall authority and influence within your marketplace. The method you use is to make sure you're seen as someone who is different ... someone who will buck the trend. By doing this, you position yourself separate and apart from the crowd. You also elevate yourself to the position of a trusted advisor who has a transformational relationship, instead of a transactional relationship, with your clients.

As soon as you start to simply declare yourself a Hit Maker—stating that you're different and better than your competitors—you almost instantly increase your ability to influence the people with whom you speak. Naturally, you will have to be able to back up your position as the go-to expert in the marketplace with knowledge and skill; however, if you're the best at what you do, that won't be a problem. The secret lies in presenting yourself differently to the marketplace than any other solution available.

As a Hit Maker, your products and services are different and deliver real value, which gives you a tremendous amount of authority within the market and the ability to influence people and the decisions they make about you and using your product or service.

Benefit #2 – Tens of Thousands of Dollars of Free Advertising Each Year

As a Hit Maker, you are able to attract positive attention to yourself from media outlets like newspapers, radio shows, television stations, etc., that are all searching for the very kind of information and content you have generated to help your prospects and clients so they can bring it to their consumers.

When your knowledge, content, personality, and success stories start influencing people and changing their lives, you become a magnet for publicity. Media outlets will hear about your life-changing efforts and will want to interview you, run stories about you, and give you coverage that would normally cost you tens of thousands of dollars (or more) if you had paid for the same kind of exposure.

As someone looking to offer your marketplace solutions, this kind of positioning will give you unparalleled credibility and authority to attract ideal prospects to your practice (and get you a boatload of paid-for press at the same time).

Benefit #3 – More Effective Marketing and Sales Messages

With a better overall position in your marketplace, your marketing and sales messages will become more effective in building an audience. Your authority and presence in the market will help your marketing get more and more interest from your ideal prospects. Your marketing and sales messages will also evoke more desire for the very solutions you are providing. Lastly, they will have more power to encourage those prospects to take action and become your clients.

The more you are seen as an authority, an influencer, and a Hit Maker, the more attraction power you will have to those you most want to serve. As a result, your advertising messages, marketing materials, and online promotional efforts will be more effective in influencing your consumers than the message from the "guy down the street" who has not transformed himself into a highly visible Digital President.

Benefit #4 – Constant Flow of Free, Word-of-Mouth Referrals

Hit Makers build large communities that are hungry for everything and anything valuable that the Hit Maker delivers. As a Hit Maker, you will change lives with each new idea and concept you share. Word of your abilities to provide value, solve problems, and change lives will spread like wildfire throughout your marketplace and around the web. Each new friend you make tells two, three, or more friends about you at the next chamber meeting and/or next civic function as well as online via social and business networking sites.

As you know, people share their best resources with their friends. To that end, you'll become the default recommendation on your topic of choice to the friends of the members of your community. That can mean hundreds more qualified prospects can come to you on a consistent basis, all for not cost to you. Imagine being able to create a slew of new clients you never had to spend a single penny to acquire. That's some serious ROI.

The result of this process means that you'll be talking constantly to high-level prospects who are already predisposed to working with you because they were referred by one of their trusted colleagues. When it comes to products and services, referrals are simply the best kind of marketing that money cannot buy.

Benefit #5 – Ability to Develop New Streams of Revenue

As a Hit Maker, you should always be thinking about expanding your scope of influence within your marketplace. You will be positioned as someone of purpose and power as well as someone who can provide new, exciting, and unique solutions for your clients.

New solutions may come in the form of providing additional products or lines of coverage to your current clients and prospects alike. Or, you may choose to offer new consulting services to your clients. Perhaps you'll want to consider moving into a whole new arena of business.

Regardless of what you choose or don't choose, the ability and choice to expand is completely within your realm of control. With a Hit Maker reputation, you dictate if, when, and where you will expand and open up new opportunities.

It's an amazing position to be in, no matter what business you own.

Becoming a Hit Maker is less about you and more about what you can do for people. The better job you do focusing on understanding life from your Ideal Client's point of view (POV) and determining how you're going to help them, the more successful you'll become in bringing a hit product to the market.

It's important to remember that the more substantial the benefits are in making a Hit Product, the more work you'll have to do to enjoy them. Bringing a hit product to the market requires planning, strategy, hard work, and obsession with over-delivering value to your Ideal Client.

The best way to communicate and deliver the value of your hit product is with a thoughtfully written book containing the stories and wisdom that make you the Digital President of your marketplace.

As you ponder what value your Ideal Client needs you to bring to the table so that you, too, can have a hit product, consider what Travis Rice felt about the impact he wanted to have on the people who watched *The Art of Flight*: "The message is an inspirational one, for viewers to get outside. That's more important than the tricks or pow slashes or anything gnarly to me," he said, "We're trying to do something good for snowboarding as a whole. Maybe we can alter someone's daily habits and get them outside every day."

Solve real-world problems in a way that it's aligned with your passion, and you're well on your way to delivering a hit product to your ideal client.

Download the **Hit Maker Manifesto** at digitalpresident.com/resources

CHAPTER 3

CORE PHILOSOPHY

———

"People will do anything for those who encourage their dreams, justify their failures, allay their fears, confirm their suspicions and help them throw rocks at their enemies."

—Blair Warren, Author of *One Sentence Persuasion*

A Core Philosophy is like a "dog whistle" that sends the perfect message to only the people you want to hear it. Much like the whistle that only dogs can hear, your Core Philosophy will resonate with, and positively influence, only consumers who fit your ICP. Everyone else will either hear and ignore it or be repelled by it and proceed in another direction.

Your Core Philosophy is defined as your belief system—your stance and positioning statement—on a set of topics, ideas, and ideals as they relate to your business and industry that you're going to use to attract and then teach your ICP how to make their business and lives better.

Michael discovered his Core Philosophy at a fairly young age while he was a membership salesperson at a major national fitness chain. When Michael got hired, he had no sales experience. In his own words, "I didn't know sales ... I couldn't close a door."

What he did know how to do, though, was to make friends. And although he hadn't read many personal development books up to this point in his life, he had read Dale Carnegie's *How to Win Friends and Influence People*.

If you've read the book, then you know the Six Principles in Part Two – Six Ways to Make People Like You fit perfectly into the sales process:

Principle 1 – Become genuinely interested in other people.
Principle 2 – Smile.
Principle 3 – Remember that a person's name is to that person the sweetest and most important sound in any language.
Principle 4 – Be a good listener. Encourage others to talk about themselves.
Principle 5 – Talk in terms of the other person's interests.
Principle 6 – Make the other person feel important—and do it sincerely.

At the time, Michael didn't realize he was 1) using these specific principles, and 2) doing what it takes to build massive rapport. He did, however, see that he was having a tremendous amount of success by using this approach to his advantage—an approach that was driven by his Core Philosophy: Be a friend first.

Michael came to see that people will do more for a friend than they will a stranger. Friends are people to whom we will sell something cheaper and make sacrifices for. Friends are people for whom we will make special considerations and for whom we will even move our schedule around.

He knew it was a powerful Core Philosophy and he used it every day to win friends (and sales).

Because of his strategy, he got to know people well during the sales process. People would tell him all about themselves, their lives, and their families. Many people would tell him everything he needed to make the sale. Some of the people he worked with even cried.

In the end, what he did was to get them to share the emotional pain that was derived from them not achieving their goal. Because of his approach and the genuine concern he showed, he earned their trust at a high enough level for them to tell him how much they needed his services. Understanding that people buy with emotion and justify with logic, he was able to influence people by simply asking questions and artfully persuading them to do what they wanted to do anyway.

He had so much success that he rose to become the number-one salesperson in the company and he did it all by looking first to make a friend instead of trying to make a sale.

Upon entering the real estate industry, he lived by the same philosophy, which propelled him to amazing levels of success by making his first $1 million over a 12-month period in only his third year in the business.

He never knocked on the front door looking to sell anyone—he went there looking to make a friend. What he learned during his time as a full-time real estate agent was that the longer he spent walking through the home with sellers, getting to know them, the easier his job was in getting the listing and selling the home.

Once, Michael took 365 listings in one year—one listing per day. Most of the agents in his marketplace who had been serving his community for as long as he'd been alive hadn't listed 365 homes in their entire career. He attributes it to his ability to build massive rapport with sellers and become friends with them before he spent one second talking about selling their home.

Your Core Philosophy Is Already Inside of You

At this moment, the wheels in your head might be spinning, thinking about what your Core Philosophy is. Don't worry about it so much right now … it will become crystal clear to you, if not by the end of this chapter, certainly by the time you finish reading the book.

Every good marketing strategy requires that a stance be taken based upon a powerful Core Philosophy.

The best news for you is every bit of your Core Philosophy is already inside you.

Here's how we know …

Michael didn't read a lot of books, have a number of sales mentors, and/or have a personal sales coach who taught him everything he needed to know about sales. He simply relied upon his Core Philosophy of making friends to guide his strategy in making sales.

In short, his Core Philosophy was already inside of him.

On top of that, once Michael got to be an expert at bringing on new members, he was given a role as a trainer for the new employees in his department. He taught them to do the same thing that he did, and ultimately they had amazing success too, even though they weren't salespeople to begin with either.

Now, does that mean every salesperson blew out their sales goals? Absolutely not. But the folks who did what Michael told them, embodied his Core Philosophy and put it to work in their daily sales activities, were super successful.

By the time Michael left, the fitness center he worked at had some of the best sales results in the company because he:

1. **Created a method** – Michael shared his Core Philosophy with the other membership representatives who worked with him and it was in alignment with how they wanted to conduct their sales efforts.
2. **Made it duplicable** – Because making friends is something that all of those people could do, it was a natural and an innate characteristic that they could tap into and have success a lot earlier in their career.

3. **Influenced people** – Michael had the kind of success they wanted and he had a solution for them to achieve it themselves.

In order for you to write a book and get people following your lead and seeking you out to help them solve their problems, you're going to need solid Core Philosophy. It's going to need to be clearly articulated and one that people can get behind and feel excited about.

When you do that, you'll be able to create a movement—a movement that is bigger, stronger, and able to reach more people than you could ever get in contact with yourself. You can create a crusade where thousands (maybe even millions) of people spread the word about you, your Core Philosophy, and how it can change others' fortunes just as it has changed theirs. Most importantly, you can create a movement that gives you the financial freedom to design a Life by Strategy so you can enjoy the life you live to its fullest extent.

How to Start a Movement

Movements are about gathering people together around a shared purpose.

In this case, the shared purpose is like-minded people who espouse your beliefs seeking you out because your Core Philosophy is in alignment with your value proposition—a value proposition that solves their biggest and most challenging problems.

What is your Core Philosophy, you ask?

Your Core Philosophy is your body of knowledge on a subject matter that clearly communicates your beliefs.

It's also the foundation for what you're going to teach your ICP based upon what they want to learn from you that's in alignment with the problems they need you to solve.

Your Core Philosophy is a result of the way you think about questions and the answers to those questions. It's also driven by what you value, why you value it, and what you think you should do when your values are challenged.

Your Core Philosophy determines your approach to solving problems and it dictates how you look at goals and the best way to accomplish them.

And your Core Philosophy is the number-one foundational element in building a movement that can change your life, your family's life, and the lives of those who choose to affiliate themselves with you.

It's important to note here that a Core Philosophy is not just a bunch of ideas—even really good ideas—that you have and share with other people. Merely having some good ideas that you share with people is not enough to formulate a Core Philosophy.

Your Core Philosophy needs to be cultivated and articulated in a way that people are attracted to it. It needs to be packaged so that they can consume it. It needs to be strong enough for people to want to follow today and long into the future.

Most importantly, it needs to be positioned in such a way that they can get excited about it, wrap their theoretical heads around it, and feel like it's filling a need or solving a problem that they have.

Owning and sharing your thoughts and ideas just aren't enough.

Are You Part of a Movement?

In the early 1960s, the Human Potential Movement took root.

The movement was based on the concept of tapping into the exceptional potential that all people possess but very few actually realize. The basis of the movement was the belief that through the growth and improvement of "human potential," humans can experience an extraordinary quality of life filled with happiness, inspiration, and fulfillment.

In 1962, Michael Murphy and Dick Price founded the Esalen Institute, in Big Sur, California. It was a center where human potential and development were studied. Esalen's goal was to educate people on the why and how of human improvement and to share ideas on the different avenues people could follow to become even better versions of themselves.

One of Esalen's students was a man named Werner Erhard. Erhard would attend retreats and seminars given at Esalen, take what he learned, and apply it to his own life. Between what he learned there and from his own study of folks like Dale Carnegie, Aldous Huxley, and Alexander Everett, Erhard experienced what he called a transformation.

Buoyed by his experience, he decided that he wanted to help others enjoy the same transformational experience he did.

This decision was the genesis of Erhard Seminars Training, or as we came to know it: EST.

Erhard's Core Philosophy was that people could transform their life if they were 1) open to the possibility that they could enjoy a better life, and 2) willing to take personal responsibility for what happened in their life and were open to being held accountable for what happened when they failed to accept responsibility.

The program Erhard created was called "The EST Standard Training" and it was a 60-hour course offered over two weekends. In the training, participants were challenged one-on-one by trainers to let go of the false persona they created from past experiences and be themselves so they could experience a rich, happy life by living each day at face value.

According to Marc Galantner, author of *Cults: Faith, Healing and Coercion*, "one study of a large sample of EST alumni who had completed the training revealed that 'the large majority felt the experience had been positive (88 percent), and considered themselves better off for having taken the training (80 percent)."

With more than one million people attending EST training between 1971 and 1984, and 80 to 88 percent of them reporting positive results, it's safe to say that EST was a huge success, especially in light of the fact that the internet wasn't made available to the public until 1991.

The story doesn't end there.

In 1991, the business was sold to the employees of the company and renamed Landmark Education. Erhard's brother, Harry Rosenberg, took over as CEO. Since then, the company has operated as a for-profit, employee-owned company.

Today, the organization is called Landmark Worldwide and it has evolved from its original format, now offering additional training and mentoring on a variety of personal development strategies.

Annually, it brings in about $85 million to $90 million in revenue from the programs and services it provides to businesses and individuals around the world.

With 46 years of operation under its belt, millions of people who have used and continue to use its services and hundreds of millions of dollars in revenue, Landmark Worldwide—and its predecessor, EST—sparked a huge, sustainable movement in personal development.

And it all started with Erhard's Core Philosophy that people can transform their lives if they're open to it and take responsibility for it.

Mental Models and Your Core Philosophy

The word philosophy comes from the Greek words *phylos* "the love of" and *sophia* "wisdom."

To have a meaningful and impactful Core Philosophy, you must continue expanding your body of knowledge—your wisdom, if you will—and strengthening the beliefs you've formed in association with that knowledge.

The broader and deeper your body of knowledge is on a variety of subjects, the more value you can bring to solving people's problems. The more problems you can solve, the larger the group of people who seek you out for your product and/or service will be.

The broader your body of knowledge, the more powerful, impactful and attractive your Core Philosophy will be.

Most importantly, the broader your body of knowledge, the more you'll be able to think like your ICP and have them identify with your way of thought.

Getting your Core Philosophy dialed in is the ultimate goal because when that happens, the door to building your community of ardent followers swings wide open and your earning potential goes through the roof.

One of the best ways to grow your knowledge base is through the learning, understanding, and use of mental models.

A *mental model* is an interpretation of an individual's thought process about how something functions in the real world. It is a portrayal of the surrounding world, the interconnection between its numerous parts, and a person's innate perception about his or her own actions and their associated ramifications.

Mental models can help mold how people conduct themselves and provide a strategy to solving problems and completing activities.

In that the key to living a Life by Strategy hinges on your ability to solve people's problems, it's vital that you learn different mental models and how they work.

Mental models are the mind's tool chest for making decisions. There are good mental models and bad mental models for every situation in life: fitness, finance, family … literally anything in life.

If you have an area in your life where you want to make changes, become a better person or become better at anything, find someone who has what you want or does what you want to do and adopt the same mental models they have. If you do, you are virtually guaranteed to get the results that they are getting.

Jim Rohn said it best: "You are the average of the five people you spend the most time with" and the mental models you have today have likely been influenced by those people. If you want to adopt some new mental models, spend some time with some new people.

The more you know about how your ICP thinks and acts, the better job you can do catering your message to what they want and need the most. More importantly, you can stay one step ahead of them and your competition, and provide value and solutions that are on the leading edge of your industry.

In order to build a solid core of mental models that serve you, you need to build what Charlie Munger says is a latticework of mental models.

Munger is Warren Buffett's partner and he's also the Vice Chairman of Berkshire Hathaway Inc.

Mental models are his passion and he believes that any successful businessperson should have a treasure trove of mental models at their disposal if they want to be a leader in their industry.

Munger believes we need to "cross-train" our minds with a large number mental models that can be used to make decisions in an infinite number of real world scenarios instead of soiling ourselves in the limited area knowledge we study in school or work.

By building a strong reserve of mental models, you'll have the tools to make your Core Philosophy easier to understand and consume. In doing this, you connect the dots for people and help them make an easy decision to start following you and consuming what you provide. Filling in the gaps is a good thing because most people don't want to have to figure things out on their own.

Here are snippets from some well-known Core Philosophies from famous people and other sources. As you read these, note how seamlessly these Core Philosophies can be transferred from the author to the audience.

- **Always Be Closing** – This famous line from the movie *Glenngarry Glen Ross* implies that everything you say to your prospect should be geared towards closing for the sale. It's a hardcore approach to sales, but it's easily understood and assimilated by the end user.
- **Become interested** – "You can make more friends in two months by becoming interested in other people than you can in two years by trying to get other people interested in you." Dale Carnegie's famous quote still rings true with the more than eight million people who have taken his class.
- **Harness your haters** – After getting slammed for her 2016 Super Bowl Performance, Beyonce sold "Boycott Beyonce" shirts on tour to capitalize on the publicity. She sold a bunch of them.
- **Never stop testing** – David Ogilvy, widely believed to be the "Father of Advertising," was the first advertising expert to use split testing as a way to test two ads to see which one would pull better. Today, split testing is a mainstay in print and digital marketing strategies.

- **Write for someone specific** – Tim Ferriss believes that you can build trust, but only when you know your audience deeply. Many believe you need to write for everyone. Ferris believes otherwise: "Write for two of your closest friends who have this problem that you have now solved for yourself."

All of these Core Philosophies are simple in their essence and widely applicable to their audience of ICPs.

Through creating a deep reservoir of mental models, you are able to hone in on a Core Philosophy that has mass appeal.

When formalizing your Core Philosophy, keep this in mind regarding mental models: They are your mind's toolbox where you go to find solutions for your and your clients' problems. As with an actual toolbox, if it's empty or it doesn't have the right tools, you'll try to fix the problem with the wrong tool and get a bad result.

It's kind of like the age-old story of the man with only a hammer. After a while, everything starts to look like a nail to him. Unfortunately, this is very narrow thinking, which is poison to a growing business. This type of thinking is not uncommon, even for successful businesspeople.

Unfortunately, it brings about way too many misjudgments and bad decisions. Many people do it every day, not even knowing they're doing it.

You likely have great ideas that you use already (you likely wouldn't have gotten where you are without them).

This is not the challenge.

The challenge is coming up with fresh, meaningful, and impactful ideas that build on your existing ideas and then taking them to entirely new levels to create cutting-edge solutions for your legion of followers.

As it relates to learning mental models and growing our base of knowledge, Parrish says: "The overarching goal is to build a powerful 'tree' of the mind with strong roots, trunk, and branches, on which to hang the thousands of 'leaves' one assimilates, directly and vicariously, throughout a lifetime: The scenarios, decisions, problems, and solutions that arise in human and biological life."

The more mental models you internalize, the more on point your Core Philosophy will be with the people you are trying to influence. Remember that.

Harnessing the Power of Your Core Philosophy

There's lots of noise out there in the business world today. The noise is the collective shouts of millions of marketers shouting, "Pick me!" to the pool of available prospects in their marketplace. Much like the roar of a screaming throng of fans at an NFL football game, it's hard for someone to pick the individual voices out from the pack to determine who is worthy of their time, energy, and money.

Your Core Philosophy, and how you position it within your marketplace, is going to determine if you get heard and how many people are going to listen and stick around.

Let's look at what your Core Philosophy needs to be and do in order for you to be heard:

1. It must provide clarity for you, your prospects, and your clients

If your prospects could solve their own problems, they wouldn't need you; they would just take care of the challenges they are facing themselves. In reality, though, not only do they not know what to do to remedy their issues, they don't know where to start.

That's where you come in. Your Core Philosophy needs to provide clarity to them—and you—as to how and why your solution is, hands down, the best one for them and their specific situation. It needs to draw them to you and make them want to stay to hear what you say, even after you've solved their initial set of problems.

What's demanded in this instance is that you articulate what's in it for them to work with you. You need to help your followers see what the differentiating factor is for you and your company and how those differences make life better for them. When you can do that, you can take on anyone, anywhere, anytime and beat them at their own game.

Just ask Steve Jobs.

Competing against Microsoft, the big kid on the block in the electronics and computer industry, was a tall order for Steve Jobs. Jobs had a tremendous amount of passion and he knew that consumers are always looking for the next big thing—the next hot trend. He saw an opportunity where he could give his crowd what they wanted by changing the way they listened to music.

Things took off from there.

It started with the iPod. Soon, it transitioned to the iPhone and then the iPad. From there came Macbooks and Mac Desktops and Apple completely infiltrated the space where Microsoft had originally staked its claim. Apple captured market share by articulating its differences and then beat Microsoft at *its* own game.

In 2010, Apple sales exceeded those of Microsoft, and they have ever since.

With a Core Philosophy of "Think Different" and a clear proposition of what they can do for their devotees that Microsoft can't, Apple has established itself as the new big kid on the block in that space.

2. It must attract your Ideal Clients and repel the rest

You can't be everything to all people, and honestly, you wouldn't want to be. To that end, you want to bring the right people into the fold while not attracting those who aren't a good fit for you.

When it comes to attracting the right people like a moth to a flame, your Core Philosophy must be articulated in such a way that you will appeal to and captivate those people who share your beliefs and values.

In the following chapter, we're going to discuss the Only One Principle. The Only One Principle deals with how and why you must craft every piece of content you create so that it's speaking to one person—your ICP.

Your Core Philosophy is the lynchpin in every idea and thought you communicate to your ICP and it's the foundation for your entire content strategy, which starts with your book. More specifically, your Life by Strategy and your Core Philosophy will ultimately dictate your entire Core Content Strategy.

The better job you do in designing your Life by Strategy and nailing your Core Philosophy, the stronger your Core Content Strategy will be, and the better job you'll do attracting the people you want into your business and life, and keep the ones you don't out.

3. It must create preeminence for you in your market

The word preeminence is defined as "passing all others." Jay Abraham has created millionaires around the globe by helping them employ what he calls a "strategy of preeminence."

The strategy of preeminence is not an approach that has you, the business owner, jumping up and down saying: "Hey, look at me. I'm the best, I'm number one" to show that you are better than others.

Rather, it positions you and your company as the expert—the expert who can solve people's problems and provide customer service in ways that your competition could never do.

The goal of your Core Philosophy is to create a preeminent business. Jay Abraham has helped business owners around the world generate billions in revenue teaching them how to master and employ the strategy of preeminence.

Businesses that are preeminent are not so because they are simply the largest or generate the most income in their niche or industry. Instead, a preeminent business is one that stands above all others in its space because it surpasses them due to the impact it has on their clients.

Abraham teaches us that preeminent businesses deliver extraordinary experiences to their customers and seek to over-deliver in this area whenever possible.

Preeminent businesses instill a sense of confidence in their buyers and hold them in the highest regard because they are committed to delivering tremendous value in everything it does for them.

When your business employs the strategy of preeminence, it takes the time to think through what it's going to do before it does it. It also leads the pack in bringing best practices and fresh ideas to the table in bringing value to its customers.

A preeminent business is one that others seek to model themselves after, collaborate with, and align themselves with for current and future endeavors.

If there is a preeminent business in a particular space, the leader of that company is looked upon as the go-to expert of the industry and the books they publish are considered to be doctrine. In other words, what they say is gospel.

A preeminent business is the standard-bearer in its industry and the one others talk about as they strive to become like them.

Again, being preeminent is not about being the biggest or the most dominant. It's about being known for delivering the absolute best experience and the most value for clients.

In short, you establish preeminence by doing what you do better than anyone else and by making a difference in people's lives when you do what you do best.

At the same time, your Core Philosophy should repel people who disagree with you.

Earlier in this chapter, we mentioned that your Core Philosophy needs to be based on your firmly held beliefs about what you stand for and the solutions you provide. You should be so unwavering in your beliefs about what you do best and how it can help people that it will make anyone who is not a good fit turn and run in the other direction.

Doing this means you are consistent in your actions and beliefs as you apply them to each and every situation.

Business development and direct marketing expert Dan Kennedy has a very particular process in how he works with his clients. His fee is not small and he won't work with anyone who doesn't follow the steps that he's laid out for them as part of his process.

When you meet with Dan, you meet with him at his house in his office. He will make time for you and you need to free yourself up for that time and make sure you don't miss that time.

Dan communicates through his assistant and through fax. If you don't have a fax machine, you will need to get one if you want to work with Dan.

Dan is not known for exchanging pleasantries and is pretty much all business when it comes to working with people and helping them find solutions for their needs. The fact that most of his books titles start with "No B.S." should give you a clear understanding of how Dan operates.

In the end, though, if you're Dan's ICP, he delivers like mad on your investment. He can help you turn hundreds into millions and do it in way shorter a period of time than you ever could yourself.

But here's the thing: Dan's not changing his process for anyone. And more importantly, he's not changing his personality or how he deals with people one-on-one for anything. As a result of this, he repels people who just don't want to work that way.

And guess what—Dan doesn't care because he knows he adds a tremendous amount of value to those who follow him and understands that he will never be at a loss for money-making opportunities because he holds true to his Core Philosophy.

4. It helps you become the Digital President of your niche

Every person who campaigns for the office of president does so on a platform. A platform is that candidate's articulation of their beliefs, values, and policies.

If you want to become the Digital President of your niche, you'll need to clearly articulate your Core Philosophy, and its associated values and beliefs, to your prospects and clients.

The clearer you are on sharing your values and beliefs, the easier it is for people to choose you now and well into the future. Your consistency in delivering your message will be the hallmark of your leadership.

Every dominant and powerful brand in the market has a clear and captivating Core Philosophy on which it's brand strategy and messaging is built:

- **Nestlé** – Good food, good life

- **Nike** – Authentic athletic performance
- **Disney** – Fun family entertainment
- **Lush** – No synthetic preservatives
- **Virgin** – Embrace the human spirit and let it fly
- **Apple** – Think different

These philosophies let you know what each company stands for. More importantly, they are clear in what they mean and it's easy for the consumer to "latch" onto one or more of these philosophies if they resonate with them.

Now, their Core Philosophy may be a bit broader in scope and definition, but the few words you see in how they represent their brand are powerful enough to move you into action.

Formulating Your Core Philosophy

How does a magician know he can pull a rabbit out of a hat? He's the one that put it in there in the first place.

It's kind of corny, but it's a good metaphor for how you're going to get your Core Philosophy out of your head (and maybe even your heart) and onto paper. You've got years of business and life experiences—as well as the assumptions, thoughts, ideas, lessons, strategies, and tactics that come along with them—that you can use to fashion an amazing Core Philosophy.

Now, it doesn't matter if you:

- Can't communicate it clearly yet
- Don't understand your audience completely
- Haven't outlined your objective for what you want your ICP to learn
- Have no method to teach what you know
- Have no formal training on how to teach
- Don't understand principles behind your Core Philosophy
- Aren't completely aware of what your ICP's problems are
- Don't have a proven structure for getting your message out the door

It's not that complex and we're going to help you get that squared away in this chapter and throughout this book.

If you want to become the Digital President of your niche, you'll need to clearly articulate your Core Philosophy, and its associated values and beliefs, to your prospects and clients.

The clearer you are on sharing your values and beliefs, the easier it is for people to choose you now and well into the future. Your consistency in delivering your message will be the hallmark of your leadership.

Here's the simple, seven-step formula you need to follow in order to craft your own killer Core Philosophy:

1. Core Desire – Define what you're going to teach based on your prospect's Core Desire.

2. Core Problems – Describe the problems that are holding them back from achieving their Core Desire.

3. Core Methodology – Deconstruct the steps to achieve the desired outcome.

4. Core Benefits – Describe the benefits or success statements of your Core Methodology, how it helps them overcome their core problems, and why each step is important.

5. Core Principles – Identify the principles that serve as the foundation for your methodology.

6. Core Stories – Identify the examples and stories that validate the principles.

7. Core Philosophy – Distill your content into a simple mental model, a statement that clearly communicates the point of your Core Philosophy.

Get the **Website Design Layout** to leverage a Core Philosophy, Methodology and Purpose so you don't waste traffic and visitors' attention at digitalpresident.com/resources

Once you've written out your ideas, beliefs, and experiences, the next thing you can do is create a conceptual model of your Core Methodology. This sounds complex, but it really doesn't need to be. It simply means you're identifying the most important components that make up your philosophy, i.e., the key concepts, words, and phrases that describe your philosophy.

Identify those components, refine them, and then draw them in a simple diagram. You can also show the associations and interactions between them. For instance, which components use other components in the diagram and how do they use them?

To have a sound and moving Core Philosophy, you need to go through describing the goal and the core problem as well as your Ideas, Beliefs, and Experiences. It sounds like a lot of work, but it really shouldn't take you that long.

At the same time, creating a simple conceptual model for your Core Methodology is not and should not be a long, drawn-out process. First time through, don't worry about perfection. It will be incomplete and it's completely normal to leave out even important conceptual components, which you will discover later when you validate your model with principles. That said, it's a worthwhile exercise for sure.

A principle is a fundamental truth that serves as the foundation for a system of belief. In other words, principles are the bedrock of your Core Philosophy.

I think it is important to reason from first principles rather than by analogy. The normal way we conduct our lives is we reason by analogy. [When reasoning by analogy] we are doing this because it's like something else that was done or it is like what other people are doing—slight iterations on a theme.

First principles is kind of a physics way of looking at the world. You boil things down to the most fundamental truths and say, "What are we sure is true?" … and then reason up from there.—Elon Musk

It All Starts with Your Book

Our Core Philosophy is simple: We believe in creating an audience and building a community around content.

No more, no less.

As we dig deeper, we can tell you that by writing a book, you can establish your authority among your followers because you're delivering value to them in the content that you provide. By illustrating your expertise and demonstrating how it can help your crowd solve their problem, you can then lead them to become your disciples (who also buy from you) in an automated fashion.

By writing a book, you can create your content and then think through the development of your Core Philosophy.

Once that's complete, you can build a funnel—your Community Funnel—that will bring all of these people into your ecosystem of content based around your Core Philosophy, your Core Beliefs, your Core Methodology, and your Core Practices about solving a problem. When you have people in your pool of followers and you deliver tremendous value to them, you now have a long-term client.

Now, you may not think you have a Core Philosophy, and it's quite possible that you don't.

For that matter, you may either think you don't need one or you're concerned that having one might put you in position to miss out on business opportunities because it requires you to have firmly-held beliefs about how to solve a problem the way you know best.

In order to be a beacon of light that people will seek out when they can't navigate the stormy seas that their problem is creating for them and in order to design your Life by Strategy where you get to do what you love, that fulfills and helps people while making you money, you're going to need to nail your Core Philosophy.

You should find that between learning more mental models and writing your book, your Core Philosophy should become very evident. And once that happens, it will provide you with a tremendous amount of clarity in what you're going to do every day of your life from that day forward.

As well, it will help you create a movement that will change the trajectory of your life and the lives of the people in your community forever.

CHAPTER 4

THE ONLY ONE PRINCIPLE

"Add as much value as possible to one person and repeat the process as many times as possible."

—Michael Reese

It was 1958 and the people of the United States were living in an era of post-war prosperity. There were a slew of luxury car options on the market at the time and the competition for the dollars of the well-to-do was fierce.

Rolls Royce was looking to run a promotion to capture some market share and it hired the man known today as the Father of Advertising, marketing guru David Ogilvy.

Ogilvy understood that all luxury cars were extremely well appointed, offered virtually every comfort you would expect from a high-end car, and were classy in every way.

His job was to find the noteworthy aspect—the benefit to the buyer—to get prospects to stand up and take notice.

As part of his research, he spent time touring the Rolls Royce manufacturing facility, met with a number of people who worked at the plant, and even drove a Rolls Royce himself.

Ogilvy knew that people of means craved a way to distance themselves from those not as well off as they are. And for them, the way they did that was to enjoy their lives in peace and quiet, away from the proverbial hustle and bustle of the average person's life.

After days of scouring everything that was Rolls Royce, he extracted what is now known as one of the best headlines in marketing history directly from the Technical Editor's write-up in The Motor:

"At 60 miles an hour the loudest noise in this new Rolls-Royce comes from the electric clock."

In the words of Gauthier, "He had struck advertising gold … the rich and famous finally had an option to escape the average, everyday lower-class world while driving from mansion to beach-home."

In his genius, Ogilvy did what everyone who wants to be the Digital President of their niche needs to do:

- Identify their Ideal Client.
- Determine what their biggest problem is.
- Decide how they would talk to them if that person was their best friend or someone else that they loved.
- Create an amazing headline that gets people's attention.
- Craft a message that resonates with them so they take action.

The important thing to remember here is you accomplish this task by thinking about your strategy and messaging at every stage of your customer's journey from only one person's perspective: your Ideal Client.

Thinking from the perspective of only one Ideal Client gives you the framework to identify how you can add as much value as possible to that one person so you can create a strategy to do that over and over for as many people as possible.

At this point, you may not have a relevant and meaningful communication strategy. Or, your approach to interacting with your prospects is ineffective because you're trying to appeal to everybody.

In either instance, your message is getting lost in a sea of platitudes instead of cutting through the clutter and resonating deeply with your Ideal Clients.

Now, all of this talk about catering your message to only one person might be freaking you out because you're experiencing FOMO, the Fear of Missing Out, on opportunities.

As you read further along in this chapter, what you'll find is that you won't miss out on any opportunities.

Not only will you attract a larger number of prospects who are ready, willing, and able to follow your lead, but also you'll still attract a large number of people who may not be your Ideal Client, who still want to follow you.

How do we know this?

Well, first let's look at *Maxim* magazine's mission statement: "We want to create a brand that celebrates men, their stories and successes, and captures the essence of men—the drive, determination, and ambition—with the fun and attitude that has long defined Maxim."

It's clear from that directive that *Maxim* magazine is a publication written for, marketed to, and directed at men (and only men).

Yet despite all of Maxim's strategy and communication efforts going towards attracting male readers, it has a readership that is 30 percent women.

If a magazine that's written for men with scantily clad women can have a third of its readership be women, anyone can focus their business on attracting a specific demographic or client profile and not miss out on other opportunities.

That said, you have to do it right in order to make it work.

And doing it right means identifying your Ideal Client Profile, laying out a path that you can take them down through your marketing and communication efforts, and then aligning your communication to the journey down that path while solely thinking from the perspective of only one Ideal Client.

By writing a book, you are able to design the journey with the right content at every turn because it allows you to think about your content in a way that seamlessly takes your ICP from where they are to where they want to be.

Identifying Your ICP and Buyer Personas

In order to become the Digital President of your industry or niche, you *must* know your ICP. It's worth noting here that there is a difference between your ICP and what is known as a buyer persona.

Buyer personas are fictional, generalized representations of your ideal customers. They speak to the different buying patterns of the companies within your Ideal Client Profile.

For example, your Ideal Client Profile may be a health care service provider with over 5,000 employees. Within that specific client profile, you might have the opportunity to work with a variety of buyer personas. Some of the people in these roles might be a mid-level manager, the head of the IT department, or even the purchasing manager. By understanding the different personas that exist, you can do a more effective job of communicating a message that resonates with the outcomes and issues that each persona is facing individually.

In all cases, you must know their wants, desires, and dreams. As mentioned in an earlier chapter, you also must know the biggest problem(s) they have that need to be solved.

In addition to that, you must communicate with them using words, phrases, language, and stories that resonate with them at a very deep level so you can cut through all the noise and make a connection with them.

The clearer you are in articulating your message to your ICP, the easier it is for them to understand and the easier it is for you to get them to follow your lead.

The challenge is, then, how do you come up with this ICP?

A client profile is a sketch you create from the confirmed similarities—not assumptions—that you identify from your audience. Your ICP determines your strategy to drive results-oriented buyer engagement (e.g. revenue).

To determine what this ICP looks like, we suggest that you first ask these three questions:

- Who are the people we want to target?
- Why will they care about what we say?
- What will we say that pertains to them?

By doing this, we can understand our prospect's point of view and begin crafting our strategy and message based upon the answers to those questions.

Being a great marketer means you understand the world through the eyes of one person's point of view: your ICP. And when you build your funnel, you'll have the marketing tool that talks just to them. The goal is to look at this from the viewpoint of your Ideal Client Profile and your primary buyer persona.

Here's how to identify your ICP so you can create your funnel for them:

- **A Typical Day** – Create a day-in-the-life scenario. Despite being first on the list, it should be done last as it's based on the remaining eight aspects of the profile creation strategy. Having this part of the process in place enables you to literally step into your customer's shoes when determining what you're going to say and how you're going to say it.

   It should include any interactions your Ideal Client has with other people during the day, as that might impact the way you speak to your customer, as opposed to if they worked alone all day. It should not be much longer than 300 words.

- **State your ICP's goals** – Be specific in what your ICP's outcomes and objectives are. Saying that they simply "want to make more money" is too nonspecific for you to sink your teeth into when crafting a specific message.

  Conversely, stating that your ICP needs to "lower their average cost per lead" would give you lots of food for thought in creating content for them.

- **Identify your ICP's main problems** – Being as specific as possible applies here, too. "Not having enough customers" would be less helpful and impactful than "doesn't have an automated, systematized customer acquisition strategy." Again, the more clearly you can identify the problem, the easier it is for you to speak to their problem and how you can solve them faster and easier than anyone else (including themselves).

- **Determine your ICP's professional background** – Be as detailed as possible in gathering information and doing research about your ICP. Understanding their skill sets, acumen, and background makes it easier for you to determine what content will have the biggest impact when engaging them in forging a relationship.

- **Identify your ICP's relevant barriers to success** – Money is a challenge for many of your prospects, but it might not be the biggest obstacle to overcome. They might have a partner, minimal experience in your industry, geographic challenges, or some other challenge that keeps them from taking advantage of your product or service. You need to know what these are in order to create content that will resonate with them. As well, always remember to consider your buyer personas as part of this process. You want your message to align perfectly with the persona that is receiving it.

- **Determine your ICP's biggest questions** – You need to identify as many questions as you can that your ICP might ask as they travel along the Customer Journey. There are different stages in the customer acquisition process and there are different questions your ICP will ask at each stage of the journey. The better you can identify those questions, the better job you'll be able to do in answering them when they come up.

- **State your ICP's preferred way of consuming content** – What's the best way to communicate with them? Do they love social media communication best or another means of gathering information? Do they prefer text? Long-form letters? Audio? IMs? What's the best tone of voice and approach to engage your ICP? Do they prefer a cheerleader or are they more driven by scarcity: "If you miss out on this, it could crush your business"?

- **Identify keywords and phrases your ICP might use** – There are certain words and phrases that your ICP will use as part of their vernacular. When you speak with them, take note of what's being said so that you can use those words as part of your content strategy to influence them properly. David Ogilvy put it this way: "I don't know the rules of grammar. If you're trying to persuade people to do something, or buy something, it seems to me you should use their language."

- **Plan out future interactions with your ICP** – Once you've gathered your information about your ICP, identify future scenarios where you'll interact with them. By doing this, you can be strategic in the content you create and the process by which you disseminate it to them. The possibilities are endless, but there will be some recurring engagement scenarios that you can master and handle with expert skill, dramatically improving your conversion efforts. What, exactly, these interactions should be will come to light as you write your book and create your Community Funnel.

By going through this process, you're able to make solid choices in the message(s) you craft and the content you create and disseminate to your ICP.

As well, it will allow you to be super clear in not just identifying your ICP, but also in what you're going to say to engage and influence them at every turn of their engagement with you.

This clarity will serve you at a high level because what you have to say will be heard by the right people, giving you significant opportunities to sell your product.

Your message to market match will be perfect virtually every time and you only need to get it right once to crush the creation of your Community Funnel.

Your Very Own "Joe the Plumber"

In 2008, Barack Obama was campaigning for President in Ohio. During one videotaped stop that year, a man named Samuel Wurzelbacher asked him a question about his small business tax policy.

As part of his answer, Obama said: "when you spread the wealth around, it's good for everybody."

Upon hearing this, the conservative media—and John McCain, one of Obama's rivals—jumped on the opportunity to portray this message as proof that Obama was interested in the redistribution of wealth and maintained a socialist view of the economy.

At the time of this campaign stop, Wurzelbacher, a member of the Republican Party, was interested in purchasing a small plumbing business. Hearing this, the McCain-Palin ticket gave Wurzelbacher the nickname "Joe the Plumber" and used him as a metaphor for the middle-class Americans during the remainder of their campaign.

The idea of "Joe the Plumber"—and even "Joe" himself—resonated with people in Ohio and even around the United States as he became a representation of the ICP McCain and Palin were looking to swing to their platform to get votes.

As "Joe" became the ICP for their campaign, they took every step they could to craft a message that spoke directly to all the "Joe the Plumbers" around the country. From that day forward, they referenced "Joe the Plumber" in speeches, debates, and interviews on the campaign trail. They even brought him in for several appearances around the state of Ohio.

In an *Esquire* article written by Mary Block on October 18, 2008, it said that

> "Joe the Plumber" has emerged as a new political force in America. During last night's debate, the phrase "Joe the Plumber" was uttered 26 times, creating a new political demographic to covet: Men named Joseph who unclog sinks for a living. While Samuel Wurzelbacher, the plumber who inspired "Joe the Plumber," may not be a licensed plumber, or someone who would be impacted by Barack Obama's tax plan, or even someone that has completely paid off his taxes, he's become an important rhetorical device.

By clearly defining who their target audience was, identifying what their main problem was and then crafting and delivering that message consistently, McCain started a huge movement in Ohio (and across America) that stoked the political fire in millions of people's hearts.

"Joe the Plumber" went from being a regular guy who didn't even own a plumbing business to a symbol that middle-class Americans could rally around in showing their desire for a sound fiscal policy by the president.

When you identify the right ICP for your business, marketing to and communicating with them is, again, like blowing a dog whistle that only your ICP will hear and respond to. Adhering to the strategy of appealing to only one person is the most powerful thing you can do to move yourself towards a fully-automated, profit-producing machine.

Navigating the Customer Journey

Now that you know your ICP and what they value the most, it's time to take them down the path from just getting to know you to being a consistent, high-paying customer. To do this, you can't just hit them over the head with "the big offer" and hope that they'll plunk down a wad of cash once they hear it.

Instead, you have to take them along what is known as the Customer Journey to build not only brand awareness, but also their faith in you and what you do. It's important to note here that you must look at the body of experiences your customers go through when interacting with your organization. Be sure to look at the entire process and provide a Customer Journey that gives a complete, meaningful experience to your consumer.

In order for you to have your customer navigate the journey effectively and end up as a loyal, paying customer, you need to be strategic in your marketing and the message you send at every stage of the journey.

In essence, you need a model on how to handle your customers on their journey in working with you.

You see, despite the fact that your ICP is the only person to whom you're talking, each individual customer is going to have different questions to be answered and needs to be met at the various stages of the Customer Journey.

Your buyer's journey is much like a story: Each one is unique in its own way. While there's no model that touches everyone the same way, that doesn't mean you should utilize some form of buyer models to augment your content marketing. Having the appropriate model for your buyer's journey adds clarity and provides additional wisdom in the creation and implementation of content marketing strategy.

To get this part right, take the time to visualize who the members of your audience are and where they are in the process of getting to know you. Ask yourself what information your consumers may need based upon where they are and which details they need to know that get them further along in the journey. The better job you do here, the more relevant your content will be to your prospects.

Having this level of clarity allows you to market with precision to not only attract your ICP, but also keep them engaged throughout the customer acquisition process.

In the next chapter, we'll discuss the Value Journey and what sort of value you would provide at each stage of the Customer Journey to keep your prospect engaged, but for the purpose of this chapter, we're going to confine the conversation to understanding the parts of the Customer Journey and the importance of being strategic in your communication along that path.

Figure 2

CUSTOMER JOURNEY & TOUCHPOINTS

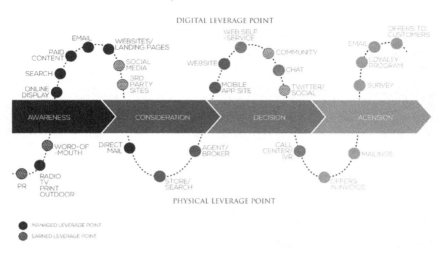

As you can see in Figure 2, there are well-defined stages of the Customer Journey process. While there is no prescribed time that it will take your ICP to flow through each of the stages, it's important that you do your job at each stage to keep them moving along.

Let's take a brief look at each stage and what it means to you and your ICP:

1. Awareness – At this point, your ICP knows little to nothing about you. It's your job to get on their radar so that you can get them to start down the path of their Customer Journey with you. The awareness phase is also what is called Top of Funnel, which we discuss in detail in Chapter 8. It's the part of the journey that speaks specifically to the problems your ICP is experiencing.

The best way to capture your ICP's attention and build their awareness of you is through a great headline. The most powerful thing in marketing is a headline because it's what makes the "call out" to your ICP as it identifies them as your target market. Headlines like these are great for creating awareness: "Three Signs Your Home Has Wood Burrowing Ants," "What's Making Visitors to Your Site Leave?," and "Which One of These Marketing Mistakes Is Costing You Money?"

It's kind of like fishing: You need worms to catch fish. Strawberries, as sweet and tasty as they are, will not help you catch fish. You need the right "bait" to get your ICP to latch onto the hook.

Your awareness strategy doesn't have to be a huge ad campaign, it could be as simple as a blog post, a text, or even a tweet.

The important thing about this part of the journey is making your headline work like gangbusters so you can catch your ICP's attention.

2. Consideration – Your ICP is crystal clear on their problem and they're looking to multiple sources for a solution. At this stage of the Customer Journey, they're considering their options and wanting to make an educated decision on who and what is going to meet their needs at the highest level for the best value.

It's your job at this phase of the process to do everything you can to speak clearly and directly to your ICP so that they hear what you have to say. When you do make the right connection, you're in great shape to move your consumer to the next step. However, failing to resonate with a prospect can mean that you could very well lose out on the opportunity.

According to the folks at McKinsey and Company in their June 2009 quarterly publication: "Faced with a plethora of choices and communications, consumers tend to fall back on the limited set of brands that have made it through the wilderness of messages. Brand awareness matters: brands in the initial consideration stage can be up to three times more likely to be purchased eventually than brands that aren't in it."

By doing your homework on your ICP and what they want and need in solving their problems, you can position yourself well at this stage of the journey to be one of the brands—if not *the* brand—of choice.

3. Acquisition – The goal of the entire process is to get consumers to make a purchase. The ease and speed of purchase will be heavily based upon the job you do during the first two stages of the Customer Journey. If you do a great job building awareness with your ICP and then make sure you "stand out from the crowd" of the carnival marketers you're up against, you put yourself in an excellent position to be the solution of choice for your ICP.

One thing that can assist you in increasing your conversion rate is the consistency of the message you deliver to your ICP along the Customer Journey.

Stenitzer mentions in his article that:

> Cognitive neuroscientist Dr. Carmen Simon found that when your message stays consistent over time, people's brains store it in their place cells. Place cells store information about things that don't move (like your home). Unlike other memory storage in the brain, place cells never run out of capacity. That's why consistent messages are much more likely to be remembered and believed than inconsistent messages. If your company uses too many different messages or changes them frequently during a months-long buying process, your brand is less likely to be remembered and believed. That makes it much harder to achieve the trust needed to close a big-ticket sale.

Fortunately, your Community Funnel provides the clarity you need to communicate a consistent, singular message.

The strategist in the McCain camp understood the importance of this principle, which helped propel "Joe the Plumber" from an unknown to middle-class icon in less than a year.

Now that's consistency.

4. Service – Once you acquire your customer, you must service them at a very high level. Servicing your customer doesn't just mean taking care of the happy ones and making sure they're enjoying your product and service. It's also about providing refunds and accepting returns, as necessary, in a timely manner.

Not surprisingly, your service strategy requires a solid communication plan too. Your customers need to know whom to call for help, how to troubleshoot problems on their own, and how to maximize the benefits of what you sold them.

Included in this strategy would be testimonials from other customers, explanations, tips and tricks on how to get better results from your product or service, and updates on any changes you made (without them having to ask). The more consistent and available your message is in this part of the Customer Journey, the happier your customers will be.

5. Loyalty – This stage is the ultimate end game, nirvana if you will, for all businesses. It's also the state where you're going to have to work the hardest to keep your newfound partners on board.

According to our friends at McKinsey and company:

> When consumers reach a decision at the moment of purchase, the marketer's work has just begun: the post-purchase experience shapes their opinion for every subsequent decision in the category, so the journey is an ongoing cycle. More than 60 percent of consumers of facial skin care products, for example, go online to conduct further research after the purchase—a touch point unimaginable when the funnel was conceived.

It's important to note here that there are two types of loyalists: active and passive.

Active loyalists not only stay with your product, they also sing its praises and recommend it to other people.

Passive loyalists, on the other hand, stay with your product because they are either lazy or overwhelmed with the significant number of other choices they have.

Passive loyalists need the most attention because they can get picked off if another brand captures their attention even for a moment. Companies like GEICO and Progressive have been doing this in the insurance industry for years.

The decision-making process for customers has very clear and distinct phases. As the Digital President of your niche, it's your job, according to McKinsey and Company, to emerge victorious in the initial "battlegrounds where marketers win or lose" opportunities: awareness and consideration.

Once you've won the mind of your consumers, it's time to move them to make a purchase and then take care of them like they are members of your family. At this point, this is where your work truly begins, as you're now required to maintain and strengthen your brand awareness with your clients so nobody else can come and take them from you.

Only a strategic communication approach will allow you to manage the Customer Journey properly where you end up with a large pool of rabid, loyal fans that hunger for your product or service.

Communicating Your Product's Value

You've got your ICP nailed and you've got a model on how to bring your customer along their journey with you and your business. Now it's time to put on your marketing hat and become the supreme Hit Maker.

Doing this means that you cater your marketing and its message to your ICP's needs in such a way that you can get them started on the Customer Journey and provide a tremendous amount of value along the entire journey.

The secret to seeing this process come to fruition is made up of a strategic messaging and positioning plan that provides a Value Exchange to your ICP for their time, their money, or both. Failing to add enough value or scaring your ICP away at any phase of the customer journey represents a lost opportunity—unequivocally.

Here's what you need to do in setting up your communication plan and then offer a Value Exchange that is juicy enough to get your ICP to take action:

1. Treat your ICP like a mouse.

A mouse has two prime directives: Get cheese and avoid cats.

A mouse will chew through a 3' wall to get a piece of cheese; however, it will run as fast as it can away from a cat in the opposite direction at the slightest hint of a whisker.

You want your ICP to chew through walls, crawl under barbed wire, and do anything else they have to in order to take advantage of what you have to offer.

To get them to do that, you must offer your ICP "more cheese and less whiskers."

- **Cheese** is what your ICP ultimately wants from you. It's the product or service you provide that solves their biggest problem.
- **Whiskers** are your attempts to sell your ICP something—even though they may need or want it—before they are ready to buy from you.

Legendary copywriter, Gary Halbert, has the distinguished honor of writing *the* most successful sales letter in direct marketing history. It was a letter about family names, the history of the name and the coat of arms that was associated with that family name throughout history. The goal of the letter was to sell the drawing of the coat of arms and the report that went along with it.

It wasn't long: only 381 words. It wasn't flashy. But it was effective.

The letter was mailed over 600 million times and it is responsible for a direct-mail empire that was sold for $90 million, years after the letter was written.

The reason the letter worked was because Halbert spoke directly to what Dale Carnegie said is the "sweetest and most important sound in any language": a person's name. It was written specifically to them and about them.

At the same time, it was non-threatening, hit on people's need for significance, gave them a reason why they should buy from him, and made them an irresistible offer.

Essentially, it had lots and lots of cheese and virtually no whiskers.

As a Hit Maker, your message to your ICP needs to be communicated in such a way that they not only want to hear it, they also want to take action once they hear it.

Communicating in a non-threatening manner that perks up your ICP's ears is the way to go as your book becomes the ultimate no-whiskers offer.

2. Employ a Value Exchange in your marketing.

The Value Exchange is exactly what you think it is: a trade of someone's time or money for something of value to that person.

Ian Stockley, CEO of Indicia, a customer engagement strategy firm, points out that a "'value exchange' between consumer and brand is one of the fundamentals of modern marketing; the basic transaction of swapping rich data for better experiences, as a means of facilitating commercial transactions and improving connection and engagement."

There are three stages of "Value Exchange" in which you and your ICP will engage at some point along the Customer Journey:

1. Gathering consumer information in return for valuable content
2. The assurance and delivery of a higher-quality customer engagement
3. The transfer of money for products or services

Your job, in knowing your ICP, is to figure out what value to exchange at which part of the Customer Journey. Ideally, the further you want your consumer to travel along the path to being a loyal customer, the more value you'll need to deliver at every turn.

The ultimate delivery of value is your client buying your product and service and then remaining a loyal customer.

A key element in creating a proper and successful Value Exchange is making sure that it's personal and specific to your ICP. The more information we gather about a consumer, the deeper we can connect with them at a more intimate level. It's this connection that drives your ICP to want to learn more—and consume more—from you.

Sir Terry Leahy, former CEO of Tesco, puts this process in a nutshell for us:

> Always look around, at customers, people, their lives, their problems, fears and hopes. Out of that empathy, the truth emerges. If you go on listening, they will give you your strategy. I never had to look for growth. I just listened to customers talk about how their lives were changing and the direction they were going in. Follow and stay close—then be the first to respond when a need emerges.

As you listen to your customer's wants, needs, and desires, you can craft responses that are extremely effective and impactful exchanges of value that are delivered at the right time and place for your ICPs.

3. Be strategic in your messaging and positioning.

Peter Drucker once noted that "there is only one valid definition of business purpose: to create a customer. The process of creating a customer is a process of communicating your vision and values to the right set of customers in the market. Your book facilitates this communication. Customers never buy just a product; they evaluate its value/utility and buy your vision."

Another way to say that your product solves your consumer's problems is called a product/market fit. A product fits a market when there is enough demand for a specific product in a large and expanding market.

According to software as a service (SaaS) entrepreneur, Myk Pono, "What we often forget is getting to product/market fit means getting to message/customer fit as well. Convincing early customers to buy is essentially testing not only how a product solves a customer's pain, but also how its value is communicated."

The message/customer fit comes about by first identifying your ICP and then sending the right message repeatedly to the ICP on a consistent basis so it moves them to learn more about your product.

It's your goal to use the right messages for the right people to create a perception about you and/or your company. By being strategic in how you position your solutions and which message you choose to send, you can create the perception you need to get people to follow you.

Then, as your ICP travels down the path of the Customer Journey with you, you have the opportunity to continue honing and targeting your message for better engagement, which should lead to strong (and more valuable) responses.

The key along the way is to provide simple, consistent messaging.

It may seem counterintuitive to craft a marketing strategy that targets only one person. After all, FOMO is a real emotion that we all experience, and honestly, who wants to miss out on an opportunity to make a sale?

Certainly, we don't.

Once you pull back the curtain on the illusion that is conventional wisdom, you'll see that what seems to make sense to the rational mind really doesn't make sense when it comes to building an automated machine that helps you become the Digital President of your industry or niche.

Focusing your research, communications, efforts, and marketing on attracting only one person—your ICP—at a deep and intimate level is what provides you with the springboard you need to create a throng of loyal clients who buy from you and recommend your services to others.

As you craft your message and employ your marketing strategy, it's vital that you match everything you share with your ICP's wants, desires, and needs ... especially as it relates to their problem. You can do this with a great communication strategy that positions you and your company in a way that will get your ICP's attention and keep it for years to come as a consistent, paying client.

Get the **Only One Principle Report** at digitalpresident.com/resources

DIGITALPRESIDENT.COM/COMMUNITY

CHAPTER 5

THE VALUE JOURNEY

"Make your marketing so useful people would pay for it."

—Jay Baer

At this point, you should be very clear on who your ICP is, what the biggest challenge is that they face, what solutions you bring to the table in helping solve those problems, and lastly, the stages your ICP is going to engage in with you along the Customer Journey.

As well, you should understand how writing a book is the easiest and most effective way to make all of that happen.

If you're not, then you must to go back and complete these steps. Without nailing these aspects of becoming the Digital President of your corner of the world, it's going to be almost impossible to complete this next task.

You see, it's time to put on your marketer hat and design the Value Journey for the funnel down which your ICP is going to travel.

In the Value Journey, you provide content and materials to your ICPs based upon where they are in the Customer Journey. By doing this, you help move your ICP along the path from where they are—which is essentially someone who is a stranger to you—and convert them into a loyal, paying customer who will be a raving fan for a long, long time.

If you're not clear as to whom you're talking with and what makes them tick, you can't create an effective Value Journey for your prospects to travel as they get to know you.

As with the Customer Journey, there is a strategy that you must follow in order to keep your ICP engaged and moving forward. The Value Journey provides lots and lots of "cheese" as a Value Exchange to your ICP for their time and allegiance to you.

The more value you offer, the more likely it is that they will want to continue learning from you and consuming what you have to offer until they make the ultimate choice to purchase your product or service (and be a long-term loyalist to you and your brand).

The key to a successful Value Journey is deciding what you want to provide in the form of content and how you deliver that value to your ICP.

If you're like most business owners, up to now you've probably subscribed to the "golden rule" of business, which dictates that you treat everyone like you want to be treated: You value them as customers and give them the best product and service you have at every turn.

With the golden rule, everyone gets the same information from you at the same time and is brought into the fold using the same approach to influence them to make a purchase.

It's a one-size-fits-all approach, and unless you're pair of tube socks, that's not the approach you want to take because it results in lost opportunities and devalues what you're providing in terms of content and product.

Conversely, if you want to have a horde of rabid fans that see a tremendous amount of value in all that you do for them—who will follow you every step of the way and take your word for gospel—you must operate by the "platinum rule" for running your business.

The platinum rule means you treat others the way they want to be treated.

With the platinum rule approach, just as with the golden rule, you still provide great products and services to your prospects and clients.

The difference is that with the platinum rule, you give each prospect what they want from you based upon where they are in the Value Journey. More specifically, it makes sure that you align your content, your offerings, and your message with your ICP's wants, needs, and desires and where they are in the Customer and Value Journey with you.

When you operate in this manner, you uncover and convert more opportunities to help others achieve their goals by working with you.

In order to build a killer Value Journey, you must understand these three things very well:

1. Every prospect has a desired outcome that they want to achieve. As such, there are clear steps they need to take in order to go from where they are to where they want to be. You must align the value you're providing to them with your communication with them along the path to that goal so you can keep your prospect moving along the Value Journey until they are ready to buy from you.

2. Every prospect will need help from you in moving forward to do business with you. You must clearly lay out their path to success in working with you and define the obstacles that might come up along the way. The clearer you are about what success looks like and what the obstacles are, the easier it is to create content to help your prospect at every stage of the process.

3. Every client will be open to a reciprocal relationship with you if you deliver enough value to them. You must be open to providing more value than you receive in return from your prospects. When you do this, you build trust and reciprocity kicks in, causing your client to continue moving along the Value Journey to an eventual purchase of your product or service.

Accomplishing these three outcomes is easier than you think it might be. That said, we're going to unpack each of them individually to ensure that you're clear on what you need to do to construct a lights-out Value Journey for your ICPs.

Desire Makes a Difference

In first chapter of *Think and Grow Rich*, Napoleon Hill tells the reader that the book contains a secret. He explains: "The secret to which I refer has been mentioned no fewer than a hundred times throughout this book. It has not been directly named, for it seems to work more successfully when it is merely uncovered and left in sight, where THOSE WHO ARE READY, and SEARCHING FOR IT, may pick it up."

If you've read the book, then you know that the secret isn't a secret at all: Before you can be successful at anything, you must want it—desire it—at a very deep level.

Desire is the catalyst that you need to drive results.

For instance, you have certain desires as it pertains to creating your Life by Strategy. Those desires have led you to reading this book and then to eventually taking action to make your Life by Strategy a reality. Your desire makes a difference in the level of success that you will achieve.

The same thing applies to your ICP.

Your ICP may desire things as well: a better life, more money, a happier spouse, healthy children, a more successful business, or something else.

As long as the desire is there, you can help your ICP achieve their outcomes through working with you. If they have no desire for change or if they don't want to seek out someone to help them affect the change they want in their business or lives, then there's nothing you or anyone else can do.

Let's take that thought a little further. Even if there are two people in the same exact situation, experiencing the same issues, the person who desires to be successful or is seeking a solution to a problem is 1) in a better position to receive help from someone, and 2) going to get better results in solving their problem.

Here's an example of what we mean:

There was a study done on two sets of parents and how they raised their children over a fixed period of their lives. The researchers found the first set of parents and gave them seven of the top parenting books to read as they raised their children.

They found the second set of parents at a bookstore who were looking for guidance in the better parenting section. They provided these parents with the exact same books and information.

After the two decades of research was completed, they sat down with the two sets of mothers and interviewed them about their experiences. What they determined was the information provided to both sets of parents was not the determinant as to whether they were successful in raising their children. What made the difference was the desire the more successful parents had in their hearts to go out and actually look for information on parenting.

Over time, the parents who were already at the bookstore looking for ways to be great parents raised better children over time and by definition, had better parenting skills.

Your ICP's desires must be present for you to help them achieve success, and you absolutely must know what those desires are if you're going to construct a powerful Value Journey for them. Because you are the expert in your niche, determining what your ICP wants shouldn't be a hard thing to define.

Pain vs. Gain

As discussed in Chapter 3 of this book, knowing what your company is and what value you bring to the table is important if you're going to provide solutions for your prospects and clients. And as a marketer, knowing yourself and what you do is that first step to delivering value.

But, you can't stop there.

Designing your marketing strategy and content from only your point of view can be shortsighted and cause you to miss out on connecting with a segment of your opportunity base.

Your view of your ICP's desires is only one view of what could be many POVs. And to that end, it's crucial you look at those, too, to get the best results for you and your clients.

We like how James Heaton, president and lead strategist of The Tronvig Group puts it:

> I would suggest that each consumer is a student, but one that is mostly a selfish bundle of desires and passions. My job as a marketer is to enlighten them to the value of my brand, and to be effective, I must start with their selfish needs. Otherwise I will not cue up sufficient interest or attention. Once I have the consumer's attention, however, I am obligated to expose them to the true value of my brand.

To "cue up sufficient interest," you need to get clear not only on what your prospects and clients value and desire, but also whether or not what they desire is a "pain" or a "gain."

Are you trying to remove a pain or trying to create an opportunity? It could be either or it could be both. No matter what, it's incumbent upon you to determine which is which.

As a matter of perspective, it's also important to note that not all pains and gains are the same.

More importantly, not all of them are the same in the eyes of your ICP.

Once you've identified the pains and the gains, you must prioritize them in order from "essential" to "it would be nice to have." This is an important step in the process of understanding the Value Journey and creating a path where you can align your strategic marketing framework with the final decisions of what content you're going to deliver to your customers and at what point in the journey they will see it.

When you do this, you can help your prospects experience the same value and service from you, but still get what they want from you no matter where they are in the process of getting to know you and their desired outcome in working with you and potentially buying your product or service.

Each of your ICPs is going to enter the journey at a different point because they have different wants and needs to be met and are experiencing different problems than others who are seeking you out for a solution.

The better you understand their desires, pains, and gains, and the better job you do prioritizing them, the more successful you'll be in communicating to them in the way they want to be communicated with.

This will ultimately lead to you being able to deliver maximum value at each stage of the Value Journey.

The Path of Greatest Success

In 1953 Sir Edmund Hillary was the first mountain climber to ascend to the summit of Mount Everest. His partner on the climb was Tenzig Norgay, a Nepalese Sherpa who was experienced in handling the rough climate and conditions one would experience while ascending a mountain like Everest.

Climbing Mount Everest is one of the most daunting and dangerous bucket-list-worthy goals that anyone can accomplish on the face of the planet. And anyone who is serious about reaching the summit knows that you must hire a Sherpa if you want to succeed.

Not only are Sherpas' bodies more acclimated to the conditions on the mountain—making them excellent guides in the face of danger—but also, their knowledge of how and where to scale the mountain can mean the difference between life and death for most climbers.

Sherpas know where the danger exists. They know when to push forward and when to sit tight. They know signs of danger in climbers' physical states so they can make recommendations on how to stay alive.

They know how to do the right things in the right order so that the people they guide have the best chance of making it the full 29,029 feet to the top of Mount Everest.

Hillary had this to say about Sherpas and Norgay: "I never regarded myself as a hero, but Tenzig undoubtedly was … the Sherpas play a very important role in most mountaineering expeditions, and in fact many of them lead along the ridges and up to the summit."

In your business, you are the Sherpa. It's your task to lead your ICP on their trip down the path of your Value Journey. It's your job to help them navigate the distance between not knowing you and becoming a raving fan. More specifically, it's your responsibility to provide them with the Value Exchange they need as they move along the path so they want to continue following it and ultimately reach the summit of their journey with you: buy your product or service and remain with you long after their purchase is made.

To accomplish this feat successfully—from the viewpoint of writing your book—there are a few things you need to do:

1. Define a clear path to success. Identify all of the situations that could arise from your ICP's point of view. That's why we mentioned at the outset of this chapter it's absolutely critical to understand who your ICP is that you're talking to and what their desired outcome is. Yes, your understanding of the path is key because you have traveled it, but looking at things from their POV is going to make a huge difference in both how you design your Value Journey and the results you get when your ICP travels it.

The clearer you are on the path and what your ICP desires, the more authentic your marketing and content will be. The more authentic those elements of the journey are, the more that what you say will impact your ICP and get them to keep moving towards the natural conclusion of working with you.

2. Create a linear path from beginning to end. Think of the layout of this path as a straight line. See Figure 3. On the left-hand side of the line you'll put your ICP and on the right-hand side you'll put your ICP's desired outcome. In between both of these points, you're going to determine all the situations, i.e., obstacles, that your ICP will encounter from the day they first meet you to the day they achieve their desired result.

Figure 3

SITUATION/SOLUTION FRAMEWORK

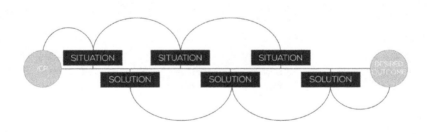

Your marketing and content creation will be centered around solving your ICP's problems (helping them overcome these obstacles). As you help your ICP overcome one obstacle, they will be encouraged to move to the next stage of the journey where the next challenge will be addressed and handled.

It's a very simple process.

This is now the path—your Core Methodology—you now own. Give it a name; brand it, and own it because it is your blueprint for client acquisition going forward.

3. Create content that evokes an emotional connection. Zig Ziglar once said that: "You're not involved in reaching your goals until you become emotionally involved." The same thing applies in you helping your ICP accomplish their goals. You must evoke emotion within them to not only grab hold of them, but to keep them moving along the path to success.

Each desire your ICP has, each challenge your ICP faces, each obstacle that your ICP needs to overcome has an emotion attached to it. As mentioned earlier, it may be a pain that needs assuaging or a gain that needs to be made. No matter what it is, there's an emotional motivator associated with it.

The November 2015 Issue of the Harvard Business Review entitled *The New Science of Customer Emotions,* provides further proof of this concept: "We consider customers to be emotionally connected with a brand when it aligns with their motivations and helps them fulfill deep, often unconscious, desires. Important emotional motivators include desires to 'stand out from the crowd,' 'have confidence in the future,' and 'enjoy a sense of well-being,' to name just a few."

Some other emotional motivators for your prospects and clients might be:

- Enjoying freedom – able to do what they want when they want
- Experiencing thrills – pleasure, excitement, doing fun things
- Feel like you belong – be part of a group; affiliated with similar people
- Feel secure – move forward in the future without worry
- Be a success in life – have a meaningful and worthwhile existence

As you look at the pains and gains of your ICP, determine what the emotional connection is on each of them. Once you do that, craft your marketing strategy and message around evoking those emotions so you can connect with your ICP at an even deeper, visceral level. That stronger connection will allow you to influence your ICP in a significantly greater capacity.

It may seem like a daunting task to lay out your Value Journey, but if you truly know your ICP and what they want and don't want, the job of laying out this path will become infinitely easier. Also, by prioritizing the pains and gains from most important to least important, you'll be able to deliver the right content in the right order along that path to get maximum results from your efforts.

Building Trust, Fostering Reciprocity, and the Free Line

Malcolm Forbes once said: "A little reciprocity goes a long way." His words are especially profound in the context of constructing your Value Journey for your ICP.

As you provide useful content to your ICP and they begin to see results in their lives and business from the value you provide, you will build trust with them and reciprocity will kick in.

Robert Cialdini, author of *Influence* and an expert on how to lead and influence others, defines reciprocity as a "rule [which] essentially states that if someone gives something to us, we feel obligated to repay that debt."

The rule of reciprocity is not a new one, as you might be aware. It dates back to 1792 when Hammurabi was the king of Babylon.

As part of his rule, he established the Code of Hammurabi, which were laws for punishment of crimes. The term "eye for an eye" was part of that code and is thought to be one of the first recorded instances of reciprocity in history.

Your goal in using reciprocity is to not only add value so that your ICP will want to "repay" you by consuming more of your content, but also to over-deliver on what your ICP expects so that they will continue down the Value Journey.

Essentially, you're creating a value account with them. On your side of the reciprocity relationship, you will continually make value deposits in the form of content and solutions to overcoming obstacles your ICP may be experiencing. On the other side of the relationship, your ICP will make withdrawals by extracting that value and using it in their day-to-day business activities and lives.

As your deposits get bigger and offer more value, your ICP will continue to come back and make the withdrawals. Their repayment to you for the deposits is the act of coming back to consume more content and eventually be a high-paying client, loyal to you and your brand.

To accomplish this, you do what is called moving the "Free Line." In the digital marketing community, the Free Line is known as delivering a tremendous amount of value, for free, upfront in your relationship with your ICP.

As you can see, it sits at the top of your sales funnel and is the line before which you will provide a tremendous amount of free, useful, thoughtful, and personally driven content to your ICP.

Your goal is to get to the point—as soon as you can—where you can move the Free Line down your sales funnel and offer for free what you used to charge people for.

When you move the Free Line, you deliver even more value than would be expected to your ICP. When your ICP sees that they can get for free what they otherwise would have had to pay money to get, you will get off-the-charts reciprocity in return and your results will start to skyrocket.

In the end, the fundamental principle here is to provide way more value than expected to ratchet up the reciprocity and make deposits in your ICP's value account.
Here's a real-world example taken from the hospitality industry:

In a study published in the Journal of Applied Social Psychology, researchers tested the impact that mints had on consumers at the end of a meal while visiting a restaurant versus a control group where no mints were provided to guests, in order to gauge their impact in increasing tips.

The results were extremely surprising (and telling at the same time):

- Group 1 participants received mints from waiters at the same time they got their check. The waiters did not mention that they were giving mints with the check; they just provided them simultaneously. This boosted tips by around 3 percent against the control group.

- Group 2 participants received two mints each from the waiters, by hand, and were told by the waiter that they were providing the mints. As well, the waiters mentioned them to the table ("Would anyone like some mints before they leave?"). Tips increased by 14 percent against the control group.

- Group 3 participants had waiters give them their check along with a few mints. A bit later, the waiter returned to the table with *another* round of mints, and made it clear to customers that they had brought out additional mints in the event they wanted more of them.

This last test saw the waiters getting a 21 percent increase in tips against the control group.

What this shows us is that by providing even more value and caring for someone, especially when it's unexpected, we can stir a tremendous amount of reciprocity in someone.

Here's even better news about reciprocity: If someone doesn't find value in your first offer, it doesn't mean you should give up in using this social rule to continue building a relationship with them.

You can make a second, smaller request of them and still use reciprocity to influence them.

How, you may ask? It's called *reciprocal concession* and it's an amazing phenomenon.
Cialdini experienced this circumstance first hand: A Boy Scout was selling tickets to an annual event for $5. He approached Cialdini to sell him a ticket, but the author declined. Realizing he wasn't going to make the sale, the Boy Scout then offered a

chocolate bar at the cost of only $1. Despite not liking chocolate, Cialdini bought two chocolate bars from the young man.

In this instance of reciprocal concession, Cialdini went from unwilling to willing when he was redirected to the smaller solicitation from the larger one.

This is important to understand because you will encounter prospects that, despite being a perfect match for your product, may be unwilling to move forward due to fear or a personal issue that's keeping them from making a decision.

When you create your Value Journey and identify the obstacles that your ICP might experience along the way, consider some smaller offers that you can make to them to keep building reciprocity and momentum moving forward.

No matter what, continue to provide a significantly larger amount of value than is expected at every stop along the Value Journey.

Building a solid Value Journey for your ICP requires some thought. In addition to knowing your ICP's wants, needs, and desires at a very granular level, you must understand the challenges they face and whether or not those challenges include them moving away from pain or towards pleasure.

Knowing all of this information is crucial, especially as you understand not only through the lenses of your experiences, but also from your ICP's point of view. Failing to take your ICP's POV into consideration in creating that path could be catastrophic and crush your marketing efforts altogether.

After you've gathered all that Intel and prioritized it, start delivering value in the form of solutions delivered via killer content. When you do, try your hardest to give your best stuff away for free by moving the Free Line as soon as you can. The result of this effort will be incredible reciprocity from your ICP to you and the foundation of a solid group of raving fans.

Get the free **Value Journey Video Training** at digitalpresident.com/resources

DIGITALPRESIDENT.COM/COMMUNITY

CHAPTER 6

THE VALUE EXCHANGE

———

"Begin with the end in mind."

—Stephen Covey

When you see the video for Dollar Shave Club for the first time, you might think it's a spoof.

But as you watch the whole thing and see that, to date, it's gotten over 24 million views, you realize it's an amazingly planned sales pitch to sell a product that's turned the razor blade industry on its ear.

Dollar Shave Club went from zero to $200 million in revenues annually in only four years and was just bought by Unilever in 2016 for $1 billion.

And yes, that says *billion*.

When you see a huge business success story like that, you have to ask yourself: "What did that company do in order to get itself a $1 billion payday?"

The answer to the question is what we're teaching you here in *Digital President*:

- Dollar Shave Club identified its ICP very clearly. They focused on a very specific market segment with a very specific problem.
- It created a tremendous amount of awareness in the marketplace for not only the problem, but also the solution that it provided.
- At the same time, its story and solution resonated with its ICP and its product and delivery method added a tremendous amount of value in solving that ICP's pain at a very high level.

Michael Dubin, the founder of Dollar Shave Club, tells us this—exactly—in his own words in a March 2015 interview with Fortune online:

> So the beginning of the story is about solving a problem for guys. And the problem that we're solving at the very basic level, and that we have been very focused on for the last couple years, has been that razors are really expensive in the store. It's a frustrating experience to go and buy them. You have to drive there. You have to park your car. You have to find the razor fortress. It's always locked. You have to find the guy with the key. He's always doing something else that he doesn't want to be helpful.

Lastly, all of Dollar Shave Club's marketing and sales were done online, where customers purchased subscriptions that automatically renew on a monthly basis.

Most importantly, in solving this problem for men who shave virtually every day of the week, they exchanged an extreme amount of value on a number of different fronts and were rewarded handsomely for doing so:

1. It's super cost effective versus the competition: Folks can buy high-quality blades and shaving accessories for a fraction of the cost—even with shipping costs.
2. It's more convenient than driving anywhere: People can order online and have the blades and accessories drop shipped to their door in a day.
3. It's a subscription business model: Dollar Shave Club makes it so that you don't even have to remember to order and pay for the blades, as they get delivered monthly after your card is charged automatically.
4. It can happen in 24 hours: Anyone who wants to start using Dollar Shave Club can go online, order blades and have them in their mailbox the next day if they want them.

And while this is an oversimplification of what happened, the success Dollar Shave Club has had leaves clues on how you can achieve wild success yourself.

One of those clues lies in the biggest thing Dollar Shave Club executed very well: the Value Exchange. If you recall, the Value Exchange is how you trade (and what value you offer) for your customers' attention and investment in you and your products and services.

How much you get in return for this exchange—and how and when you offer the exchange of value—rests in nailing the business model you choose for your enterprise.

Your business model is what allows you to capture the value you create.

In defining and implementing your business model, you're going to want to make sure that it is 100 percent congruent with your Life by Strategy so that you don't sacrifice your style of living and quality of life simply to make sure your company makes money.

Your goal is to maximize that value and make the exchange happen automatically to get Monthly Recurring Revenue (MRR) flowing in the door.

You'll do this with a solid revenue model (or models) that works in conjunction with your business model to collect the income on the value you exchange.

In order make sure you implement the best business model and maximize your Value Exchange, you're going to need to determine the Total Addressable Market (TAM) for your business and do the math on how many/how much of your product and services you need to sell to fulfill your promise to your customers and still be congruent with what you want in your life.

There's no brain surgery here, just the process of doing the right things in the right order so that you can live your Life by Strategy and have a business model that serves your and your client's needs long into the future.

Selecting the Right Business Model

Peter Drucker defines a good business model as one that provides answers to the following two questions: "Who is the customer?" and "What does the customer value?"

By now, you should have an excellent idea of who your Ideal Customer is and what value you bring to them in your specific industry.

You chose an ICP because you have an idea of the type of people you want to do business with and you created a Life by Strategy to determine the life you want to live.

However, if you're like many business owners, you likely didn't make a deliberate decision about the model you chose for yourself. In fact, there's a good chance you modeled it after someone else's business or took the suggestion of another person.

As well, there's also a strong likelihood that your business model isn't aligned with your Life by Strategy so that you can solve your ICP's problems and enjoy the life you truly want to live at the same time.

Despite all that, you might have an opportunity to create revenue through a myriad of strategies and approaches to delivering that value to your ICP.

But you need to know that when it comes to your business model, not all revenue is created equally.

If your business model is not aligned to your ICP and does not let you live your Life by Strategy, you aren't going to get the results you want.

Having a business model that's not in alignment with these two things is like climbing a ladder that you have leaning against the wrong wall.

What will happen is that you'll end up in a business where you're creating the wrong kind of customers—customers that you hate to work with.

And you'll be killing yourself—hating every minute of it—just to make a buck.

Again, not all revenue is created equally.

Revenue from a misaligned business model is not the kind of cash flow that comes easily and consistently to you like a business model that's in alignment with you and your ICP's goals.

In the end, having the wrong kind of business model—the kind that doesn't give you the full value for the services or the products that you provide—will be disastrous, painful, and likely not profitable.

To that end, you need to work from the belief system that your business model supersedes any strategy you have in place. What that means is you can have the best strategy in the world to make money, but if your business model isn't right for your ICP and your life … you will not be maximizing your revenue opportunity to its fullest capacity.

Michael learned this first hand in 2010.

He was running a successful coaching business. The coaching was high ticket, but it did not scale easily and he was unable to serve a large set of the target market. He had a clear buyer persona that he could deliver a ton of value to, however, he had to find another model for delivering the value that would keep the margins high and hopefully solve the scalability challenge that you run into when you're building a large coaching or consulting business.

In his research to find a solution to his problem, he ran across what is called a continuity sales model from an info product he purchased.

A continuity sales model is where a buyer purchases an initial product for themselves or their business and then they enter into a subscription agreement where they continue to receive products or information from that company with their payments being taken automatically from their credit card, debit card, or bank account.

When he saw this, he realized that he, too, could offer a tremendous amount of value and information on a monthly basis to real estate agents across the United States and Canada from all the materials he had created for his real estate coaching program.

Over time, he had created hours and hours of recordings from topics he spoke on and interviews he conducted with industry experts. He also had scores of scripts, dialogues, white papers, and systems and strategies he had documented in hard copy that he could provide to people.

Having all of these components of the program already created, he was able to design a magazine that offered some robust digital collateral along with it for agents to consume.

It was the perfect opportunity because it gave him the chance to create MRR and align the project with activities that he was already doing.

His challenge in creating the model was to determine if it was going to be delivered in a digital or hard copy format. He also had to create the perfect funnel in order to attract the right people who would be willing to pay the fee he was charging for the program. The costs of doing all of that played heavily in how he rolled out the concept as did the kind and quality of the material he included in the program.

All of that mattered in delivering on his promise so he could get the best results.

After a tremendous amount of legwork and brainpower was expended, Michael launched his funnel.

To track his sales, Michael used a software program that sent him an email with the words: "Cha-ching, a sale was just made" every time someone paid for a subscription to his magazine.

The cha-chings rolled in fast and furious that first day, and within 24 hours he had 255 people who became online clients of his, willing to pay the monthly fee for his magazine and information. The number of enrollees grew to 1,800 people in a very short period of time after that.

The great news is that business allowed him to get the core revenue to be able to cash flow a marketing department that would organize content and support the company's additional business opportunities. The business model started as an info business and then the info business leveraged into a continuity sales model. And through that continuity and subscription strategy, he was were able to roll out other businesses, including hiring coaches to help grow coaching, getting paid consulting gigs, and eventually doing large, high-ticket conferences and seminars. And it all started with the core audience that he was able to build through the membership subscription he created.

There are pros and cons to every business model, especially as it pertains to creating your Life by Strategy. It's important that you weigh all of them when selecting the best model for yourself.

To help you determine which business model will work best for you, your ICP, and by extension, your Life by Strategy, let's review some of the different online business models out there that you can use to create consistent, automatic income—much of it in the form of MRR from subscriptions just like Dollar Shave Club.

Here they are in no specific order:

Affiliate Marketing – As an affiliate marketer, you sign up and agree to sell other people's products through a specific channel or to a specific audience using websites you built around those products or services. Virtually every product or service imaginable has some sort of affiliate sales program associated with it. Some people have even devised businesses around helping other people manufacture affiliate offers and then attracting affiliates to those offers. It's called creating Affiliate Networks. Still, other people have even built businesses around categorizing and organizing Affiliate Networks to make it easy for entrepreneurs to find them all in one place.

Drop shipping – Drop shipping is a great entry-level exposure to the ecommerce business model. Rather than spending a load of money on building your own inventory that you will eventually need to house and then sell, you build a sales funnel that identifies buyers for products that can be drop shipped directly from the factory or manufacturer. Your profit margins aren't as robust as in other models, but if you're just getting started or if you're a marketing genius, you can use this model to grow a large, successful business.

E-commerce – You can think of e-commerce as a digital retail store. With e-commerce, you purchase products, inventory them in your own facility and then and fulfill orders for those products. You will promote your "store" via a variety of internet marketing approaches and strategies. The majority of e-commerce entrepreneurs out there use pay-per-click traffic to find buyers for their products. You can also combine e-commerce and drop shipping to help reduce inventory costs when opening your store in the beginning. It allows you to see what products work best and it even gives you the opportunity to white label some products for your store itself.

Software as a Service (SaaS) – SaaS products are on fire right now and they are extremely profitable. And, since virtually every SaaS product has an ongoing billing feature, SaaS product owners can take a bit of a loss on the initial sale and still make a profit over the lifetime of repeated software usage by the customer. SaaS products give small businesses the opportunity to compete with large IT companies without the large IT company cost associated with employing a large number of developers and building their own software. SaaS products are in virtually every niche out there today.

Information Products – If you're interested in making money online, then you've likely purchased a video, e-book, or other product online that showed you how to do it. The market for info products extends much further than just "how to make money online." It's a huge industry. Any product or service where you can teach somebody how to do something they want to learn how to do can be an info product. The best part about information products is that once the product is created and the work is done, you can grow your info product business as big and as wide as you want it to be. And, other than the marketing costs you'll incur online, it's a pretty cost-effective way to make serious money online for the right individual.

Apps – Creating apps is a huge business. There are over two million apps in use as of the writing of this book, and there's no limit to the number that can still be created and sold for money. And, the more addictive you make your app—Tinder, Snapchat, Instagram—the more people will use it once they download it (instead of filing it away in some folder on their phone's desktop). If you have a knack for making things entertaining while keeping the material fresh and interesting, creating apps may be the choice for you.

Freemium Model – This is a combination of "free" and "premium" and it's been a popular strategy used by startups over the last decade. The model offers a simple product or service to customers for free, while charging for premium services (upgraded features and perks) to paying members. It's important that if you choose this model that you find a good balance between what you give for free so that users will still need or want to upgrade to a paid product or plan.

Productized Services – If your company provides an online product—writing, editing, graphic designing, SEO, pay-per-click, web design, etc.—this may be the model for you. Rather than having one job that gets so large that it eats up all your time, you can sell packages of products and services to customers and then create "add-ons" to make the packages more lucrative to you and more valuable to your client. It also allows you to customize what you do for people, which gives you the ability to monetize your product or service even more.

Lead Generation – Lead Generation (Lead Gen) is where we have done our best work. If you have the ability to provide a lead source to your ICP and help them grow their business exponentially, you can make a tremendous amount of money in this vertical. The best part about this opportunity is that you can serve a number of clients in the same industry (even in the same marketplace) and continue to make money on a regular basis. You can set up levels of the leads you provide based upon the quality of the lead and charge a premium for better-qualified leads. What's even better is that you can have your leads ready for purchase—or produce them in very short order—to fill your ICP's needs in a quick turnaround time.

You know your ICP and what they need and want from you. You also know your product line and the value you bring to the table. It should be fairly obvious which model will be most congruent with your needs and the needs of your ICP.

If you're still having some trouble determining which business model is for you, you may want to utilize a business model canvas. A business model canvas is a strategic management template you can use to create a new or document an existing business model. It is a visual blueprint with aspects that illustrate your product's or service's value proposition, framework, customers, and finances. In using a canvas, you can create a tremendous amount of clarity as to which business model will serve you, your company, and your ICP best.

Download the **Business Model Canvas** at digitalpresident.com/resources

As part of your business model vetting process, you should answer the following questions to get maximum clarity when making your choice:

- Who's your ICP?
- What would cause your ICP to start seeking a solution to their problem?
- What are the meaningful features and benefits (FaBs) of your solution?
- Who and what are your ICP's alternate selections for a solution, including your competitors, making no decision, and solving the problem themself?
- What's the classification of your solution? Does it fit into a category?
- What's your unique value proposition? What sets you apart from other solutions?
- How will you reach your customers? What's your strategy?
- How much does it cost to make a sale and what are your revenue models?
- How will you determine if your business model is successful or not?

Some of them you've already answered through the activities in this book. Some of them you haven't. To be clear, you must know the answers to all of these questions in order to implement the ideal business model for your situation.

Maximizing Your Monetization Strategy

Once you've determined which business model is best for you, you need to determine the means by which you will collect revenue from your clients. To do this, you'll need to select a revenue model or models that fit your needs best.

Here's a quick review of the predominant revenue models in use today:

1. **Transaction revenue** – The one-time sale of goods or services. You are likely engaged in this strategy to make money and realize that it does not lend itself to creating MRR.
2. **Project revenue** – You perform a one-time project for someone and get paid. Again, this model is not conducive to generating automatic, consistent income.
3. **Recurring revenue** – In this scenario, your client pays for continued access to a product or service on some sort of pre-agreed-upon payment schedule, often monthly or yearly.
4. **Service revenue** – You provide a service to your client and in turn, your client pays for time or expertise. This model can provide for MRR if you set up the payment plan for your services accordingly.
5. **Freemium Offer** – You offer your prospects something of value for free and then convert them to either a one-time higher purchase or to a subscription model.
6. **Advertisements** – You sell ad space and get paid for the sale. In some cases, you can work out a payment plan to get MRR when someone wants to continue advertising in the same spot(s).
7. **Marketplace** – Online retail income where you have a platform or marketplace to bring buyers and sellers together. In this model, you could charge a monthly fee to sellers in order to consistently expose their products to buyers.

The great news about revenue models is that you don't have to have just one in place. For instance, you could start with the freemium model to pique someone's interest in your product. Once you have them on board, you can upsell them to a recurring revenue program and collect MRR from them for months or years to come. There's really no limit to how you can interconnect the various revenue models available to you.

Our goal for you is to create a business model that allows you to put yourself in a position to collect MRR on a month-over-month or year-over-year basis. We want your revenue to be automatic and independent of your ongoing sales efforts. When this happens, you are in the best position to live your Life by Strategy.

At this point, you may be asking: "Why all the fuss about business models?"

It's a great question; here's the answer: The business model you select will ultimately have an impact on how much your business will be worth if you ever want to sell it.

Here's what we mean.

A couple of years ago, Michael met with a guy who was the CFO of a billion dollar company. At the time he was evaluating another company's business and what

Michael saw shocked him because he had no idea how valuable that company really was. To Michael's surprise, it was way more valuable than he had ever thought—way more valuable than anyone would think in light of the revenue it was producing.

That company was RentJuice, a rental relationship management service for landlords, property managers and rental brokers that helps them market their inventory and client relationships. At the time, it had around 14 employees and was doing $30,000 a month in revenue while being used to manage about one million rental units.

The shocker was that despite the smaller size of the company and the moderate revenue it was producing, RentJuice was gobbled up by Zillow for $40 million.

It was at that moment Michael realized it wasn't the company size or revenue that drove the company's valuation, it was the business model. It was how the company captured value and then capitalized on its ability to do so.

Here's some even better news.

Once you get clear on what the best business model is for you, you can start to look outside of your business to see how your model can complement (or be complemented by) other businesses, customers of other businesses, and even vendors that exist in your industry.

It's called the Value Net (figure 4) and it's a way for you to put the results your business model gets on steroids.

Figure 4

THE VALUE NET

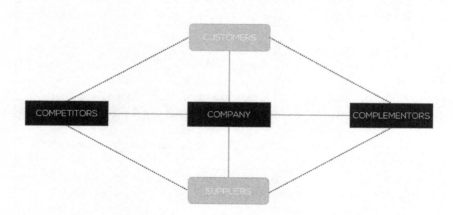

The Value Net has you take a look at the different players in your business and industry to see what ways you can either learn from or cooperate with each of them to 1) add more value to your current customer base, 2) find additional ways to bring on more customers, and 3) increase profits.

Rather than employing a "dog-eat-dog" mentality, the model encourages cooperation with the other key figures in your industry to help you expand your market and opportunities.

However, only through understanding your ICP, the value you bring them, and having the right business model in place are you able to leverage the Value Net to experience exponential growth in your own business.

If you'd like to find out more about the Value Net Model and how to put it to work in expanding your sphere of opportunities, check out *Coopetition* by Adam Brandenburger and Barry Nalebuff.

Having the right business model not only means the difference between success and failure for your own enterprise, it also can mean the difference between millions and billions when and if you are ready to sell.

Maximizing Value Serves Everyone

The whole purpose of becoming the Digital President of your industry or niche is to create the life you desire while serving others at a very high level.

It's about contribution and fulfillment all at the same time.

The challenge for all of us lies in creating the delicate balance between working and living our lives to the fullest. Even the President of the United States—the most powerful person on the face of the planet—takes time to golf and go on family vacations.

He has to or he'll be eaten alive by the huge weight that rests on his shoulders each and every day.

That's the benefit of a Life by Strategy: You get to do what you love to do, help others, and give yourself the gift of time in the process. And when you provide a boatload of value, you help others and yourself even more.

More importantly, the more quickly you can get your consumer to appreciate and consume the value you create, the more money you can make for yourself.

The key to making all of this happen, though, is making sure your business model is in alignment with your Life by Strategy. If what you do every day to help others and make money is congruent with what you want each and every day to look like, then you are in a position to have an amazing, fulfilling life.

Conversely, if you're working your tail off and getting little to no fulfillment—even if you're making great money—you're not living a Life by Strategy.

We know this not just from our experience, but also from some of the great businesspeople with whom we associate every day.

Earlier on in our business, we had an affiliate partner selling our products who was a really good speaker. His business model was this: If you put him in front of a room, he could sell anything. At the time, he didn't have a strategy and he definitely didn't have a Life by Strategy outlined for himself.

What he did have, though, was a solid mental model which was: "You've got to earn your stats." What he meant was that if you're going to be successful and put up big numbers, you must work hard—very hard. The model worked and he used that line to get the attention of his audience no matter where he spoke.

His goal was to sell others' products and to build an audience to whom he could market and sell in the future. He didn't have his own audience, so he was using an affiliate model to sell our product as a way of getting in front of people to create one.

To accomplish his goal, he went from town to town, brokerage office to brokerage office, and city to city. Trust us when we say that this is a very expensive and labor-intensive way to build a list.

Certainly, our guy was adding a tremendous amount of value to other people, but he wasn't really capturing a lot of it for himself to make his life better.

He worked hard and spent most of his time on the road. It was tough on him and his family.

We remember having a conversation with him one time and what stood out wasn't the success he was having. It was how he was managing his constant traveling.

He shared with us how he had devised the perfect suitcase and how he packed it so he could be ready in no time. He shared his strategy as to how he didn't have to stand in line when he got to the airport. And, he talked about how he and his wife had a system of picking him up and dropping him off at the airport. He even had a strategy on how he picked out his rental car.

What he had become was a very savvy business traveler and he built his business and life around that. What he hadn't accomplished was building a Life by Strategy where he wasn't trading his time or money for money.

He wasn't living life by design, he was a road warrior.

You see, he modeled his approach to business—his business model if you will—after his mentor, another successful trainer and sales expert in the industry. This gentleman, we'll call him Tom, had been doing workshops around the country for 10 years. He had a huge name in the industry and what he taught changed people's businesses and lives forever.

Unfortunately for Tom, as much as he was having success on the road, he was failing in his own life. He was not a happy person. As well, he was always away from home, and as such, he had a troubled marriage and strained relationships with his family.

Tom's story has a tragic ending because instead of making the changes he wanted and needed to make in order to live the life he deserved for helping so many other people, he took his own life at the age of 45.

Tom left his wife and two children behind.

Our affiliate saw this and realized he needed to change his business model—even if it meant modeling someone else. You see, he was married and his wife had child. They both wanted more children and he just didn't want the same life that Tom had.

He wasn't willing to sacrifice his current family and not have additional children just to keep his business going. He saw the incongruence between what he was doing and what he wanted in life. As a result, he attacked the strategy of how he was going to create and capture value in the marketplace.

Once he did that, he wound up building a product he could sell and service from home. He already had the audience, so he had a group of followers that he could easily market the product to in a short period of time.

And because he made that change—that crucial decision to live a Life by Strategy and add massive value to both his customers and himself—he is now making way more money than he ever made on the road. And he does it all from the comfort of his own home, traveling only when he chooses to.

Weighing the Pros and Cons

There's another part to our affiliate's story that we didn't share with you. You see, he didn't just wave a magic wand and turn his life around.

Since he had such a tough time with the first business model he replicated, he wanted to make sure he didn't make the same mistake again. Along the way to figuring out what was the best long-term solution for him, he looked at modeling some other people's approach to their businesses to see if worked for him.

At one point, he was hoping to get into the software business. To execute that strategy and business model successfully, he started studying other people that did what he wanted to do and eventually modeled someone he knew to be super successful in that space.

When he jumped in a second time, what he saw, once again, wasn't what he wanted. In the person he was modeling, he saw a person who had 60 employees (he had a handful). He also saw a huge commitment of time and energy. Yes, he had way less time on the road, but he still wasn't working from home and making a ridiculous amount of money through selling high-margin products and having satisfied customers.

He ended up hiring a bunch of people and even getting an office—the only time he's ever owned an office—and tried to make this second business model work.

He was making great money, but it still wasn't what he wanted.

In the end, he decided to create products that could be sold and consumed online—automatically. He set up a subscription model for his business and started hauling in MRR at the fastest rate he had ever experienced. The best part was that he had time for his family and ran his life and work on his own terms.

In a strange turn of events, we found out that his products were so good and beneficial to the end-line consumer that we signed up as an affiliate of his and started selling them online to our base of customers.

The moral of the story here is that you just can't pick any business model. It has to be in alignment with what you and your ICP want. Any old business model won't do.

To that point, when you're modeling someone else, you just can't look at the model they have in place.

You have to weigh the pros and cons of the model based upon what your Life by Strategy looks like. You need to look at what it takes to support that model from the perspective of your resources of time, energy, and money. You need to see what kind of commitment it's going to take to make that model work.

You must know deep down what you're saying yes to before you make your decision. As we said earlier, you don't want to climb to the top of the ladder only to find out that the ladder was up against the wrong wall.

Understanding Your Total Addressable Market

The last thing you need to do before you go in "whole hog" on implementing your business model is to put pen to paper and understand the financials behind your decision.

Here's what you need to know to make the best decision from a financial perspective:

First, you must know how big your opportunity is by determining your Total Addressable Market or TAM, as we explained earlier. Your TAM is the universe of prospects whom you can market to in an effort to secure a business relationship at some point in the future.

When Woods was running his short sale business, he originally wanted to market directly to investors whom he thought were the hungriest for the leads he could provide them. For him, the TAM was originally the pool of real estate investors in the United States.

As time wore on, he expanded his horizons and started looking at the total pool of real estate agents across the country, a much larger group of prospects.

Soon, he started looking at his business as if he was servicing the 1.1 million realtors that were registered to sell homes in the United States. That entire pool of agents was now his TAM. His business model decisions were made based upon the belief that he had the opportunity to get every single realtor in the country on his platform.

In your world, you want to expand your horizons, too. You always want to start with making sure that the Total Addressable Market is large enough for you to be able to hit your goals in terms of customers and revenue.

The next thing you need to do is create a model to understand the unit economics for your product or service to fulfill your promise to your ICP. The best way to start this part of the process is by asking yourself: "What is my goal? What's the target I'm trying to hit?" It may be that your goal is to make $100,000 a year or maybe it's a $120,000 a year. Maybe that's $10,000 a month. The amount doesn't matter, you just need to know the number.

Once you do that, you need to verify some assumptions on what it will take to hit that goal: How many customers would you need to have? If you want to make $10,000 per month and your customers are all paying you $1,000 a month, you would need to have 10 customers.

Knowing that, what's it going to cost in order to generate those customers? How much is it going to cost in order to service those customers? This model is based on you verifying assumptions that you've made about how much you want to make, how much it will cost to deliver your product or service, how many people you need in order to hit your goal, how much you'll make per sale, etc.

Then, you can take it even deeper by chopping up all of the different ways that you can deliver your product or your service. What are the different price points at which you can offer your product? What are the different ways to collect the money? Is it a product that gets you MRR or is it a high-ticket, one-time transaction?

This story should tie this chapter up into a nice bow for you.

About a year ago, we started a consumer-facing lead generation platform. Before we set out to make it a reality, we went through the same process: We had some original assumptions and we looked at the Total Addressable Market. At the time, we believed that the product could actually deliver opportunity for real estate agents to tap into the first-time homebuyer market, which at the time that we launched, consisted of 50 percent of the marketplace.

Our TAM for the project was based on about five million real estate transactions or roughly 2.5 million first-time home buyers. We knew without a doubt that the market was big enough for us to be able to generate a large number of leads of first-time home buyers.

Originally, we based our model on being able to sell data to our clients and then provide them with the tools to be able to refine that data, generate sales leads, and ultimately create customers.

As part of our offering, we created territories based on our data models that would identify people who were renting a home. In knowing that data, we were able to reverse engineer when these renters would be a potential homebuyer based on various factors: their credit score and when their utilities were connected. This information allowed us to pinpoint within three months when they would be coming up for a lease renewal and if they were in the income level that would be able to purchase a home.

As with all new ventures, flexibility was the key to success moving forward.

We generated a number of sales at the price point we had picked and we sold people the tools and data they needed in order to fulfill our promise to them. What we found is that our clients had a hard time creating their own ads and refining the data using the tools we provided to them.

Seeing this, we decided that it would in the interest of our clients to help them get to the value faster, and it would be in our best interest to move up the Value Exchange by doing exactly that.

So, we did exactly that.

We started running all their ads for them and then drove traffic to our site to generate leads and provide them with a high-quality lead that has already been to our site, requested help in buying a home, provided their contact information, and is now waiting to be followed up with by a real estate agent.

This shift in our model allowed us to increase our sales price and revise our territories based on the fact that we were now providing the leads.

Also, by shifting our model from pivoting off of data and how much data was out there to determining how many leads were in a territory (and how many agents could work in each territory) we were able to move up the Value Exchange even faster. Consequently, we were able to deliver more value faster and charge more for the service.

It was a huge win-win for us and our customers.

As you start delving into business models and monetizing your business, remember to adhere to this mental model: It's not about pulling the trigger, it's about hitting the target. So many people say they don't have time to plan and do things right, but they always seem to find the time to do it over when they get it wrong the first time.

Selecting the right business model is as important as anything else you're going to do in making your business successful. As you do your research, remember that you might have to start with one business model and make some adjustments along the way until it's perfect for you, your business, and your ICP. And above all else, make sure that whatever you end up with, it's in alignment with delivering maximum value to you and your ICP at every stage of delivering that value.

See how you can achieve your financial goal and buy your time back. Get the
Person Freedom Model at digitalpresident.com/resources

CHAPTER 7

AUTHOR-ITY

—

"Be an authority on a subject with influence, or be subject to the influence of an authority."

—Woods Davis

In June 1883, the magazine *The Chautauquan* published the now-famous philosophical question, "If a tree were to fall on an island where there were no human beings, would there be any sound?" It's kept scientists and philosophers busy debating the true answer for years, and to this day there's still no definitive answer.

We have a similar question when it comes to building a brand and driving sales for a product: "If you have an amazing product or service, the best fulfillment strategy for said product or service, and can get better results for consumers than anyone in your niche, but you're not known as the go-to authority in that space, will people choose you over your competitors?"

The answer here is much clearer: absolutely not.

The good news, though, is that no matter what level of celebrity you have (or don't have) in your marketplace, that can be changed. You can get the consumer's attention—and keep it—if you employ the proper strategy.

Our philosophy is that no matter what niche you're in, you can establish impenetrable authority and effortlessly attract a consistent stream of high-value clients who will buy your product, become raving fans, and remain as long-standing members of your community. With the proper level of authority, you will have a tremendous amount of influence over people and be able to get their attention better than any one of your competitors.

David Goggins is a perfect example of this.

Goggins is a retired Navy SEAL and an endurance athlete known as the "Toughest Athlete on Earth." In fact, if you Google "Toughest Athlete on Earth," his picture and about a half a million search results about him pop up. He's absolutely one of the most resilient people we've ever met and our encounter with him was a life-altering experience.

We initially learned about Goggins in the latter part of 2016 while we were on a snowboarding trip to Colorado to talk some business and enjoy one of our favorite pastimes.

One of our goals when we travel is to read at least one book during the time we're away. And historically, we read books that either recommended to us or that are written by people who would have a high level of influence with us because their story rings true with who we are.

On this trip, we decided to read *Living with a SEAL: 31 Days with the Toughest Man on the Planet.* This book captured our attention for two reasons:

1. The author of the book is Jesse Itzler, a super-successful entrepreneur who is, among other things, the co-founder of Marquis Jet (which was acquired by Netjets and is now owned by Berkshire Hathaway), a partner in Zico Coconut Water, and a part owner of the Atlanta Hawks. His wife, Sara Blakely, is also a super-successful entrepreneur as she is the founder and owner of Spanx Inc., the shapewear giant that specializes in foundation garments that contour the body. Blakely's net worth is $1 billion.

2. The story is about Itzler and Blakely's decision to have a Navy SEAL come live with them for one month. The key here isn't that it was just a Navy SEAL; the key was that this SEAL is known as the toughest athlete on the face of the planet, both mentally and physically. In addition to being an American hero, he broke the Guinness World Record for pull-ups in a day—he did 4,030 in 17 hours—and he ran 100 miles in under 19 hours despite never having run a marathon of any kind before.

The Core Philosophy of the book is that once you think you're done performing an activity—that you've reached your threshold for mental and physical pain—you're actually only 40 percent done. You have 60 percent more to give, so you need to push your mind and body through the pain to get your actual pain threshold.

Goggins is the SEAL in this book and his accomplishments as a Navy SEAL and an endurance athlete are incredible and inspiring at the same time. However, if his story hadn't been shared in this book, we'd have never known about him. Fortunately, we do and his authority is strong with us and tens of thousands of other people around the world.

He is truly the Digital President of his niche and a perfect example of how authority and influence work together.

The Toughest Athlete (and Digital President) on Earth

As it is, Navy SEALs are some of the toughest—if not *the* toughest—humans on the planet.

Just to be considered for the brutal Navy SEAL training program you need to swim 500 yards in 12:30 (10:00 rest), do 50 push-ups in 2:00 (2:00 rest), 50 sit-ups in 2:00 (2:00 rest), 10 pull-ups in 2:00 (10:00 rest) and run 1.5 miles in 9:30. In addition to that, there's Hell Week, which the Navy describes as: "5 1/2 days of cold, wet, brutally difficult operational training on fewer than four hours of sleep."

Goggins has successfully completed Hell Week two times, something most other SEALs only do once.

It's all an insane test of physical and mental strength and it's a huge part of the entrance exam into the most highly selective and elite platoons in all the Armed Forces. At the time of the writing of this book, there were only 2,450 SEALs on active duty (less than 1 percent of all Navy personnel).

The more we consumed Itzler's book and the more we learned about Goggins and his message of pushing yourself beyond every limit you think you have, the more authority he had with us. He was someone we aspired to be like, someone who had demonstrated that he had achieved amazing results like finishing 135-mile runs in under 30 hours on multiple occasions, completing the Kona Ironman World Championship in under 12 hours, running 100 miles in under 24 hours, and running 205 miles in 39 hours.

If that isn't inspiring enough, he achieved all of that—and more—despite overcoming challenges like being 100 pounds overweight at one point in his life, having asthma, being bullied physically and psychologically as a child, and having a congenital heart defect that went undetected for years.

His internal fortitude comes from his mantra: beyond motivated.

What he accomplished was of significant interest to us. We're alpha males who pride ourselves on pushing our minds and bodies to the ultimate edge of what we do in life. We subscribe to the philosophy that effort is the energy that it takes to overcome resistance and that if you want to do something, it's going to take 10 times the effort in the gap between where you are and where you want to go.

This book was a spot-on match for who we are at our core, and Goggins had our full attention.

Seeing this, we sought to find out everything we could about him: where he came from, what his life was like, what his Core Philosophy was—we wanted to learn it all. We had to know who he was.

He had serious authority in our eyes.

Imagine having a message so dialed in and your ICP can hear your story so clearly that they would go through the trouble of trying to find out your name and everything about you.

In the book, there were a lot of great stories about how SEAL—that's how Itzler refers to Goggins in the book due to the fact that he didn't want his identity revealed—pushed Itzler way beyond his mental and physical ceiling.

One story in particular impacted us so strongly that not only were we compelled to duplicate it in our own lives, but also, we influenced someone else to join us.

On a frozen, five-degree day in the dead of winter, 2010—after a 10-mile run in a blizzard—SEAL took a boulder and cracked a hole in the ice on a lake on which kids were playing ice hockey. SEAL jumps in and tells Itzler to join him in the freezing-cold water of the lake and stay there until he tells him to get out.

Hesitant, Itzler plunges barefoot into the waist-high section of the lake as SEAL commanded him to do. After a few minutes, SEAL tells Itzler to get out, not worry about putting his sneakers on, and run barefoot in the snow to his house before frostbite kicks in.

Itzler knew that SEAL's reason for doing this was to "test his mental toughness muscle." We wanted to do the same thing, so we took it upon ourselves to face and overcome the same challenge.

On that same trip to Colorado, we were relaxing in the natural hot springs located near the resort where we were staying. In the area adjacent to the spring, there was a river and the water temperature was approximately 19 degrees at the time. It wasn't frozen because the water was moving at a pretty good clip, but it was frigid.

Because Goggins's authority had influenced us so strongly in the book and because we aspired to be like him, we decided to hop into the river. And, because we felt so strongly about doing it and were so committed to doing it, our authority transcended beyond us as we were able to influence our friend Todd Abrams—founder of Icon Meals, an IFBB Professional Bodybuilder, and an overall physically and mentally tough gentleman—who joined us in the icy waters of this river.

The experience was amazing and surreal at the same time.

When we first read *Living with a SEAL*, we were unaware of how wide and deep Goggins's authority had already spread. But as we started to seek him out on Facebook (approximately 100,000 followers), Twitter (roughly 90,000 followers), Instagram (about 90,000 followers), his personal website, his podcasts, and other places on the web, we came to realize that he was already famous with extreme athletes, people who aspire to get more from themselves and their lives, and with people who are in alignment with his "never quit" mindset.

We saw evidence of all of this, first hand, in the spring of 2017 when Michael was at his son's taekwondo class. That day, Michael sat down next to the father of one of the kids in the class. His name is David Miller and he's a financial planner in North Texas.

Prior to this meeting, Michael and David Miller had never really had a substantive conversation other than saying hello to each other and making small talk. On this occasion, David asked Michael a single question: "Have you heard of the book *Living with a SEAL?*"

At that moment, Michael had instant affinity with David Miller and he realized how powerful Goggins's celebrity was.

Remember, David didn't ask: "Do you know SEAL?" or "Have you ever been in a cold river?" or "Can you run a hundred miles?" or anything else related to the book.

He asked that one question and Michael immediately bonded with him—instantly.

You see, authority is one of the most powerful principles of influence. If you go back to your childhood, you probably remember doing some things you normally wouldn't have done because you were under the influence someone who had tremendous authority with you.

For example, one night in 1992, Michael saw the famous rapping duo, Kris Kross, on *The Arsenio Hall Show*. If you don't remember them, their trademark was that they wore their pants backwards as part of their act. He was so influenced by the authority the duo had on him that the next day, he went to the skating rink with his pants on backwards.

No joke.

What most people fail to realize is that the influence of authority still works on us just as powerfully today … especially if it's congruent with our aspirations and outcomes. Certainly, it explains why three totally sane and healthy men would jump into a freezing-cold river in the dead of winter with a hot, bubbling spring only yards away.

David shared how he was under the influence of Itzler and Goggins's authority and their story.

As it turned out, David knew someone who was bringing Goggins into North Texas to work out, and we had a chance to work out with him.

At this point, Goggins had reached legendary status in our eyes. And once we found out that he was coming to town and we had the chance to not only meet him, but also work out with him, we were on fire to learn everything we could about him.

In addition to doing all the research we mentioned earlier, we went back and read every one of his Instagram posts, looked at his posts on Facebook, and the history of what he tweeted online again. We even went and found articles we hadn't read, and watched a boatload of videos. Michael even sent SEAL a video on Instagram letting him know how SEAL had impacted his life and how excited he was to meet him.

We even recommended the book to everyone in our sphere. Some of these people had become rabid fans like we are and they were excited to meet him too.

The excitement and anticipation were palpable.

On the day of the event, SEAL didn't disappoint: he ran 10 miles as a "warm-up" to come work out with us. As expected, the workout was a beast. But that's not what stood out for us.

What stood out was the level of influence and celebrity SEAL had with the people who knew about him. You could see it in people's eyes: They were excited to meet and work out with him.

He was larger than life in person, but not just because of his accomplishments. We all know someone who has accomplished some amazing things in life. We were all so influenced by him because of the book, the story, and the legend that was created because he was positioned as the expert in what he did.

Michael connected with him at an even deeper level because he grew up in a military family (his mother was a command sergeant major). As a result, he had to move a lot as a child and start over from "scratch." He built a tremendous amount of resilience from having to overcome the challenges that came along with that.

Like we said earlier, meeting him was a life-changing experience.

The best thing about it, though, is that in addition to changing the lives of the people who consider themselves members of his loyal fan base, he's impacted the lives of the children of fallen servicemen from around the United States. Through his celebrity and through his efforts, he has raised awareness resulting in more than $2 million for the Special Operations Warrior Foundation, which gives college scholarships and grants to children of fallen special operations soldiers.

Goggins's purpose is to help others believe that they can overcome any pain, challenges, or obstacles they've faced in the past, and even those that they face now. This cause is in complete alignment with who we are and how we want to conduct ourselves. His purpose inspired us so deeply that we want to do everything we can to help him help his charity.

Remember, all of this happened 1) because we read Itzler's book, and 2) because he and Goggins established a tremendous amount of authority, which allowed them to influence us (and others that we knew) at the highest level.

Establishing Authority is Key

There's no mystery in how to create authority in your marketplace. You position yourself as an authority by consistently disseminating practical, useable content to the members of your audience—content that comes from the book you've written.

The information that you share in this content needs to solve their problems, provide solutions, and meet their needs. You get people's attention because you position yourself as the expert who is willing to share your expertise, teach them what you know, and be an advocate in helping them achieve their goals.

As part of your positioning strategy, take a specific stance on what you believe to be true and do not waver from it. Your goal is to be polarizing so that you can attract the people who want to work with you and repel the people that don't. Doing this helps you build the community of raving fans you want and need to create your Life by Strategy.

In short, if you want to be an authority and have influence in your marketplace, you need to write a book, use the content from that book to grow your authority, and become an authority and content marketer throughout the process.

Here's why:

Let's say you're trying to decide between using one of two accountants to lower the tax burden for your small business.

Accountant #1 has been in your area for a long time and is part of a business networking group of which you are both members. He seems sharp and has a good grasp of what you need to do to accomplish your goal. To boot, he's a really great guy.

Accountant #2 is a best-selling author on minimizing taxes for a small business and he is regularly featured on the local news about changes in the tax law. Plus, he also publishes a blog where he clearly teaches how his strategies work and demonstrates the results his clients have achieved with his system.

The choice is fairly clear at this point for most people.

Is Accountant #2 particularly smarter than Accountant #1? Will he get you better results because he's a published author and does television appearances?

Unequivocally, no.

That said, Accountant #2 will be able to generate more income, bring on more clients and do both consistently because he has positioned himself as an authority.

He is the go-to expert in the market.

It's much the same with David Goggins.

There are thousands of current and past Navy SEALs, many of whom are famous in their own right. As well, there are tens of thousands of extreme and endurance athletes. For these reasons, Goggins has authority just by being a SEAL. He also has authority just by being a successful endurance athlete.

But, by combining his expertise and experiences from both backgrounds and then providing consistent content like podcasts, videos of workouts, blog posts, Facebook, Twitter, and Instagram posts, he has established himself as the ultimate authority in his niche of endurance athletes and people who want to push themselves beyond their perceived limits.

Not only does he have thousands of followers and members in his community, he is a highly sought-after speaker, regularly requested guest on talk shows and podcasts, and the topic of thousands of articles and blog posts.

His authority speaks for itself and that's what you want for your company, your brand, and yourself.

Seven-Step Strategy to Creating Massive Authority

There's a strong possibility right now that there aren't enough people that know you in your market. As a result, it's hard for you to establish yourself as the authority for what you're best at doing. As we mentioned earlier, in order for you to have that clout with the members of your audience, you need to grow your legend—expand your brand, if you will—by getting and keeping their attention.

Your authority isn't just about you and who you are; it's also about the benefits you provide to your followers as a result of your authority. TM Schwab/Online Business Accelerator shares some insight on authority as positioned by Sonia Simone, co-founder and Chief Content Officer of Copyblogger Media with Brian Clark. Her understanding of authority is helpful:

1. **Authorities serve their audiences.** Zig Ziglar said, "You will get all you want in life if you help enough other people get what they want."
2. **Authorities genuinely know their stuff.** There's a lot of junk out there. If you can provide beneficial information which is easily accessible, you will have authority.
3. **Authorities care.** People instinctively know when you care. There's no gaming this process.
4. **Authorities are strategic.** Show how your expertise and authority can help others translate their effort into building their business.
5. **Authorities take the long view.** Shortcuts take far too long. The long game generates success.

There is no brain surgery here, otherwise we wouldn't have been able to do it for ourselves, and certainly, we wouldn't be able to teach it to you. Here are the seven steps you need to follow to make yourself a celebrity in your marketplace:

1. **Identify your specialized field of knowledge** – Identify your position in your marketplace in relation to your target audience around your specialized field of knowledge. Where do you currently stand in the mind of your target audience? What subject matter do you want to be an authority on? What business opportunities would you have if you were known as the go-to authority on your subject matter?

   As you are drilling down to your specific area of authority, note the distinctions in your areas of expertise. For instance, you could be a head coach for a football team or you could be a position coach. Both are coaches, but their areas of expertise are different. Both have specialized knowledge, but not in the same area. You need to align your specialized knowledge to the opportunity. The more specialized you are within your niche (and even the smaller the niche), the easier it is to stand out and resonate with your audience.

2. **Have a clear and polarizing positioning statement** – Your positioning statement is a one- or two-sentence statement that articulates your product or service's unique value to your customers in relation to your competition. In determining your statement, you need to ask yourself: "Who is the target market that I serve?," "What's my magic power/specialized positioning strategy?," "What do I stand for and what do I stand against?" Your goal is to have a polarizing voice in the marketplace and all your positioning is going to be geared around those three elements of your statement. All of your messaging will align to your positioning statement. Clearly define what you stand for, what you stand against, have your messaging align with it, and have a positioning statement that sums it all up.

3. **Align your brand to your positioning statement** – Goggins stands for being beyond motivated. His positioning statement is very powerful and it

gets people to take action: "Everybody comes to a point in their life when they want to quit but it's what you do in that moment that determines who you are." He is an authority on running, extreme endurance, and pushing beyond limits, even though he was a Navy SEAL before he was any of that. He took his experience and expertise and aligned it to a very specialized niche. And, because he has such authority in that niche, his influence is incredible.

Since we read the book, we registered, and are now training for an ultramarathon in the form of a 60-mile race. When you craft a brand identity that is congruent with your positioning statement and clearly represents what you stand for, that's when you create amazing authority.

4. **Document your Core Content** – Document your Core Content on the subject for your target audience and align your content to your business objectives. To accomplish this objective, you need to document your Core Stories, Core Philosophies, and Core Methodologies and align them to the problems your Ideal Client will look to you to solve. The good news is that as you write your book, this material will not only be created, but it will be organized in a manner where you can use it effectively to build authority with your audience.

5. **Build your content machine** – To establish and maintain authority, you'll need to implement a system that continues to produce relevant content for all forms of consumption preferred by your ICP. You'll use your Core Content to create articles, videos, podcasts, and other forms of media to reach your audience. You'll also create content that simply shares your point of view on the current subject matters that are relevant to your audience. Your content pieces are the cogs in the wheel of the machine.

Your goal is to choose content that reinforces your brand while at the same time solves the very same problems that your clients are trying to solve. You should commit, in your calendar, to creating content on a regular basis so you always have material to use.

6. **Build your content publishing system** – Goggins produces regular, live workouts as part of his content machine. His community is desirous of workouts and plans that increase and test their fitness on a regular basis. It keeps them engaged with him and excited about what's going to come next. As part of this process, you should also commit to a content publishing schedule that requires you to publish at regular intervals. Remember, authority only comes if you provide consistent, fresh information to your followers.

7. **Start your movement** – As we discussed in Chapter 3, you're looking to create a movement that will build a massive community of rabid fans who will follow you into battle … who will tell everyone they know and love about

you, what you've done for them, and in turn, what you can do for their friends and family. Your community is a place where like-minded individuals gather together to share a common purpose. As with a physical community, if you designate an outlet online where members get together to share common interests and engage with one another, you will form a bond with your members that extends beyond business. Grow your community and your authority will increase.

The best way to establish your authority, even in today's digitally driven learning environment, is to write a book. Not an e-book, but an actual book made of paper with words typewritten in ink and a front and back cover.

As of 2015, the Pew Research Center shared that 72 percent of American adults read at least one book a year with the average number of books that Americans read each year being twelve.

And, to boot, 12 percent of Americans will consume a book by listening to it.

It's safe to say that book consumption is still strong. It should not come as a shock to you that the word authority has the word "author" in it.

Authenticity and Authority

Being authentic means that you share the real story, you share the real you.

Business growth and marketing expert Dan Kennedy says that when you're on stage, "You share your story." If you went bankrupt, tell your audience you went bankrupt. If you were sexually abused, then let your audience know.

Some of the most influential people we know share their real story with their audience. The best people we have followed are amazing at telling the "Hero's Journey." And these people are multi-millionaires who have thousands and thousands of followers.

They don't hide behind it, they embrace it: the good, the bad, and the ugly. And as a result of that, they are authentic in communicating to their audience and their audience connects with them at a very deep level. If you've been to prison, investigated by the FTC, or if you were homeless or addicted to sex, crack, or alcohol, it's incumbent upon you to be authentic and tell your story to your ICP.

It's the same reason that Goggins has so much authority. He's overcome a ridiculous number of obstacles in his life—many challenges that others have faced or are facing—and he's extremely credible and authentic when he shares his story of how he did it.

When you take this authenticity and write a book sharing your expertise and your story in overcoming obstacles that others have faced or are facing, you, too, can establish incredible amounts of authority, and you differentiate yourself from your competitors.

The awesome byproduct of your efforts is that you have an amazing marketing tool that can help you expand your influence and broaden your sphere of opportunities as wide and as deep as you'd like to go.

What's even better is when you write a book about how to solve your ICP's biggest problem, you deliver massive value to your ICP. The more value you create and your ICP consumes, the more authority you have. The more authority you have, the bigger your ability to influence and persuade your Ideal Client.

For instance, when we knew SEAL was coming, we started consuming everything that he had available for consumption. Also, as we partook of what he provided to us, we were thinking that if he recommended the sneakers he was wearing, we would have bought them. If he had suggested certain workout clothing, we would have bought them. The same thing would have happened if he had shared what nutritional supplements he used.

We were taking in everything he had to offer, we were ready to follow him wherever he took us, and that's what you want your followers to do.

It's a proven formula and one you'll want to put to work as part of designing your Life by Strategy.

Influence and the Client Journey

As we stated earlier, you just don't "get" authority—and the opportunity to influence the members of your audience—you have to earn it.

Your client's attention is not free.

As you recall, they are going to experience a Customer Journey and it's your job to influence them along the way so that they not only keep moving the along the path, but also to get them to consume more and more content from you and eventually make a purchase of your product or service.

Being able to influence your prospects and clients is so important because the more content you create that they consume, the more influence you have over them. It's a powerful compound effect that you can create in moving your prospect from not knowing you to being a raving, long-term loyalist for you and your company.

Influence expert Dr. Robert Cialdini, whom we introduced in Chapter 5, has identified six laws that govern influence. He maintains that influence is neither magic nor luck, rather, it's science.

As a marketer, you need to understand the science behind influencing others if you are going to experience any success at all.

Here's a brief look at all six laws.

Law 1: Reciprocity – We introduced you to this law in the previous chapter and talked about how your ICP will go over and above to continue following you and consuming your content as you deliver more and more value to them. Reciprocity simply refers to the feeling of indebtedness someone feels to us when we do something nice for them or give them a gift of some sort of value. Reciprocity is always at play in your strategy of influencing your consumers.

Cialdini believes that as marketers, we must make the first move. We have to give something: information, free samples, positive experiences, etc. We have to give people something of value so that they want to give us something in return. Reciprocity is a central element of the Free Line concept, as you remember. The more we move the Free Line up on higher-valued content and materials from our business, the stronger the reciprocity will be from the members of our audience.

Law 2: Social Proof – Consumers will always look to other consumers—especially those that they know—when making a purchasing decision. It's how we got sold on SEAL and his Core Philosophy (we took Itzler at his word in his book) and how our friends got excited about SEAL by what we had to say about him. How else do you get five of your friends to the gym for one of the hardest workouts of their lives?

Law 3: Commitment and Consistency – Loosely translated, do what you say you're going to do, and do it regularly. You must deliver the goods to your consumers when you say you will if you want to have the power to influence.

Law 4: Liking – People want to do business with those that they like or they think are like them. You and your ICP share similar pains, pleasures, and experiences. The more your ICP likes you or feels as if they are like you, the more they will follow your lead. Be sure to key on these aspects of your relationship with your consumers.

Law 5: Authority – This one is the "big daddy" of the group and why we're spending so much time on it. People have respect for authority and they desire to follow the lead of someone with it. Authority—and even the appearance of it—increases the chance that others will comply with someone's request. In order to lead people and effectively influence them to take action, you must have authority with them.

Here's an example of the power of authority: Several years ago when he had established himself as a beast listing houses in Frisco, TX, Michael was traveling in the Seattle area visiting his family. While there, he checked in on Foursquare, a popular social media app at the time, letting people know where he was.

He instantly got a text from an agent in the area that knew about him, Jeremy Mellick. Jeremy is a friend of ours and we work with him now.

We did not know him back then.

The text said: "I would be willing to pay you a thousand dollars an hour for as many hours as you'd be willing to spend with me tomorrow morning."

After chatting with his wife and assuring her that she could use the money to buy herself a purse or whatever she wanted, Michael firmed up his time with Jeremy.

The next morning, Michael met Jeremy for breakfast and Jeremy handed him $2,000 in cash.

Again, Michael didn't know Jeremy and Jeremy only knew Michael through what he had read and seen about him online. But that day they met up, spent two hours together, and Jeremy paid him $2,000 for his time.

That's the power of authority.

Law 6: Scarcity – This one is pretty simple: the less quantity there is of something, the more people want it. This law can be overused, especially in marketing, so you'll want to use it wisely. The good news is that if your product or service solves your consumer's problems faster than anyone else's can, scarcity may be a great friend to you in your influencing efforts.

Being able to influence people with eloquence and elegance is a science and even an art form. The key, once you identify your ICP, is to deliver your content to them on your platform using influence as the rudder to direct them along the customer journey.

If you recall, there is a decision-making process that your ICP will go through before they determine what market research expert, Gigi DeVault, identifies as their "level of involvement" or what we know as the "final decision."

DeVault states that: "Many choices that consumers make about brands, products, or services are mid-level decisions that require only limited problem solving. The higher the perceived risk of a decision to a consumer, the more effort and time the consumer is generally willing to put into a structured or expanded decision-making process.

And the more time the consumer puts into the decision-making process, the better job you need to do in influencing their choice to be you and your company.

DeVault confirms the five-step decision-making process (Buyer Journey) for us:

Problem recognition – Sometimes consumers realize they have a problem and they go about searching for a solution. Other times, a solid advertising and/or marketing campaign will bring the problem to light, causing them to search for answers. In either case, you need to provide the right headline(s) and content to grab and keep their attention at this phase of the journey.

Information search – Your consumers will do a tremendous amount of research at this time to evaluate solutions and gather information either in support (or not in support) of the solutions they find. You want your information to be easy to find and valuable to them as they start aggregating data.

Evaluation of alternatives – At this point, there will likely be a considerable number of alternatives. It's vital for you to do an amazing job at leading your prospects towards considering your solution as being the best one for their specific needs. They will, in this stage of the process, start narrowing down their options as to who and what is the best provider.

Product choice – When it comes time to make a decision, consumers will start to use heuristics to refer to their trusted mental models to make faster decisions so they can move forward in solving their problem. Heuristics are things like country of origin, brand loyalty, and the belief that paying more for a product means you're getting higher quality, i.e., you get what you pay for. How your consumer views your product in light of these filters is heavily weighted in your ability to influence them.

After-purchase evaluation – This is where the hard work kicks in. Your now-clients will consider any buyer's remorse they are experiencing and do an informal review of their satisfaction and/or dissatisfaction with your product and the decision they just made. At this stage of the process, it's crucial that you continue to influence your clients on how great of a purchase they made and give them tons of value on how to benefit—even more—from having your product or service at their disposal.

DeVault maintains that there are multiple "internal and external influences" at play throughout all the steps of your consumer's decision-making process and that it's important to consider all of them in your strategy of leading them down the path:

Internal influences include many of the attributes that are embedded in target market segmentation efforts, such as lifestyle, age or generation groups, attitudes, personality, level of education, motivation and perceptions. External influences include situational and social factors, such as time, the physical environment, culture, subculture, social class, gender roles, group memberships, opinion leaders, and trendsetters.

Your ability to pay attention to, and address, your ICP's wants, needs, and desires in relationship to these internal and external influences will exponentially increase the results you get in leading them to their eventual buying decisions.

When you understand what drives your ICP and create content that speaks to their heart—to their soul—you will get people to do things that you would never believe they would do along the Customer Journey to working with you.

The Power of Video in Influencing Others

Video has been a huge part of how we've captured people's attention, attracted them to us, and then gained influence over our audience. It allows us to control the narrative in a unique way and lead people in the direction we want them to go better than almost any medium out there.

Getting your consumer's attention is the first major step in influencing them to follow and then decide to work with you. In fact, it's one of the most difficult parts of marketing your products and services.

If you were a superhero in the marketing world, your super power would be your ability to get someone's attention.

And whether you're looking to grab someone's attention so you can sell your book as part of your marketing strategy or if you want to get them started on the Customer Journey on the way to scoring a copy of your book, video is an amazing way to take hold of—and keep—their attention.

According to video marketing experts WireBuzz, when you use video, you don't have just one super power, you have four: attention, emotion, perceived value, and clarity.

1. Attention – Animoto says a product video is 4 times more likely to be watched than read about in text.

Forbes states that 59 percent of executives say they prefer video to text.

Marketing Sherpa reports that video doubles time-on-page.

Capturing someone's attention is a crucial first step in customer acquisition and certainly a step in the overall process that you want to crush when start building your funnel.

2. Emotion – When you can touch on more than one person's senses at one time—especially sight and sound—you dramatically increase the chance of connecting with your prospects in getting them to take action. According to ComScore, video increases email click-through rates by 200–300 percent and 64 percent of people say they are more likely to buy a product online after watching a video about it.

3. Perceived Value – Overall, people perceive video content to be more valuable than written content. It's not that written content isn't good, because it is. It's just that video is harder and costs more to produce. Plus it takes more time and people realize this when they consume it. People will allocate more time to you and your company, provide more of their contact information, and even pay a higher price for your product as a result of consuming your videos.

4. Clarity – We've been stressing consistently the importance of clarity in delivering your message. With 65 percent of the population being visual learners and another 35 percent of it being auditory, video is the perfect medium for connecting with and reaching your audience faster and with more clarity.

As you can see, getting people on board the train—and keeping them on board—is extremely important if you want to have a solid chance at influencing them on any level. At the same time, you must understand how to lead someone effectively and use the science of influence to create massive amounts of authority with them to accomplish that. A solid use of video in the right places will help you make that happen faster and easier.

Engineering Influence With Content

If you want your content strategy to properly and effectively drive your consumers where you want, when you want, you need to plan when and where you're going to place your content.

As well, you'll want to make sure you employ all of Cialdini's six laws of influence to ensure that you do a sufficient job moving people all along of the spectrum from being a stranger to you all the way to being a soldier in your army of believers.

Daniel Newman, CEO of Broadsuite Media Group and expert at bringing together technology and the human experience, maintains that the content you need to produce for your customers is highly dependent on what stage of the purchase process they are currently experiencing: brand awareness, brand affinity, or purchase intent.

With those three stages identified, Newman believes that there are three types of content you need to produce:

1. Expert Content (third-party content which they defined as credible)
2. Brand Content (from the brand or brand employees)
3. User-Generated (reviews such as Yelp or Amazon)

Now, expert content carries a tremendous amount of weight in influencing consumers to make decisions at all three phases of the buyer process. But when you peel back the layers of the onion, you can see how each type of content has its own set of strengths at each level.

Brand Awareness – Expert content has the most strength at the beginning of the purchase process. Consumers trust expert content the most at this stage of the game because they are gathering information and believe experts are the "go-to" people during this segment of their buying journey.

At this stage, the laws of reciprocity and authority are crucial. Authority will grab your consumer's initial interest and reciprocity will keep them coming back to consume more of what you offer. Again, the more content you offer that your ICP consumes, the more trust you will have and the more influence you will be able to exert over their choices.

Brand Affinity – As your consumer becomes more familiar with you and your company, they want more content from the brand to strengthen familiarity, which builds trust in their minds. Expert content is still great here and should be used, but brand content is important to consumers here.

In this phase of the process, you will definitely want to employ the laws of liking, commitment and consistency, and authority. You want your consumer to identify with your brand so strongly that they feel like they are your friend or family member. As you deliver your content consistently to them, they are certain to feel more strongly that your product or service is the right one for them. Lastly, sprinkling in the law of authority keeps your consumer feeling like you are the one true solution for their needs.

Purchase Intent – Customers are influencers too. Once someone decides to make a purchase—or has made a purchase—they have a tremendous amount of trust for others who have done the same. Newman points out that: "Many tend to think reviews can deter purchases but it appears that once a buyer is close to making a purchase they are more willing to overlook negative reviews."

At the time of purchase (or the intent to purchase), the law of social proof is crucial. You need to let other success stories do some influencing and selling for you. The law of liking is also key here because people want to do business with those that they know, like, and trust. Great messages of success with your product or service will get fence sitters into the game. And again, the law of authority will help you cement purchases and give your clients the strong feeling that they made the right choice.

Knowing where your ICP is in the buying process and understanding what makes them want to make a buying decision will help you with what content to provide at what interval of the journey on the whole.

The better job you do with this part of the process, the better position you are in to be the true Digital President of your marketplace. Consumption of the content you produce is massive as you have the opportunity to disseminate your materials through a variety of different channels: blogs, videos, emails, texts, on social media, and everywhere in between. As your consumption increases with the members of your audience, so does your authority.

It's an incredible phenomenon and it all starts with writing your book.

One last thing about engineering influence: You can never have enough social proof, case studies, testimonials, or demonstrations about your business and the solutions it provides.
The people who buy your products and services and see you in action are just as much influencers on your ICPs and future buyers as you are as the expert.

Take the story of Elisha Graves Otis for example.

Name doesn't ring a bell? It should, especially if you live in a multi-story building with an elevator. Otis wasn't the inventor of the elevator, though you probably see his name on elevators around the world. What he was, though, was the first guy to convince people (read: influence them) that he could create an elevator that could not just go up, but also go down without breaking into a freefall.

We take this for granted today, but back in the mid-1800s, this was a big deal.

Otis only sold three elevators for $300 his first year in the business. During the first few months of the second year, he sold none. Knowing he had to get people's attention in order to make a sale, he set up a demonstration at the New York Crystal Palace, a magnificent exhibition hall that was constructed for the 1853 World's Fair.

Otis Elevator, the company, depicts the historical event his way:

Perched on a hoisting platform high above the crowd at New York's Crystal Palace, a pragmatic mechanic shocked the crowd when he dramatically cut the only rope suspending the platform on which he was standing. The platform dropped a few inches, but then came to a stop. His revolutionary new safety brake had worked, stopping the platform from crashing to the ground. "All safe, gentlemen!" the man proclaimed.

Otis, the man, achieved the desired result and sold seven elevators that year. The next year he sold 15 and although he passed away seven years later, the company, then run by his sons, had 2,000 elevators being used.

Once they had the proof, Otis Elevator got orders to have their lifts put in the Eiffel Tower, the Empire State Building, the Flatiron Building, and in the original Woolworth's department store, which at the time was the world's tallest building.

They even installed all 255 elevators and 71 escalators in the World Trade Center.

In 2017, Otis Elevator, now 164 years old, hauled in $13 billion in revenues.

And none of it would have happened if Otis the man hadn't done as Cialdini recommended and made the first move, which led to the demonstration and proof that he needed to launch his product into the future forever.

Again, you can never have enough proof, testimonials, and demonstrations for your business—no matter in what phase of the buying journey your consumers are currently involved.

Know What Makes Your ICP Tick

Our original fascination with Goggins began with us picking up a book written by a ridiculously successful businessperson. We wanted to know why someone who didn't have to do anything that he didn't want to would expose himself to someone who was going to tell him what to do, when to do it, and how much of it to do—anytime on any day for a full month.

As we read the book, we came to not only appreciate the author, Itzler, and his desire to test himself and push the limits of which he thought he was capable. But what captured us was the man who took Itzler on that journey of self-discovery—David Goggins.

Not only did Goggins solve a problem for Itzler, he solved a problem for us. We wanted to push ourselves harder. We wanted to know what was on the other side of "I'm done" and "I can't go any further."

And through him, we discovered that.

On one podcast, what he said hit Michael between the eyes. For Michael's entire life prior to being exposed to Goggins, he worked out with people and used to love to watch them hurt. He would do insane workouts with people—even when he didn't want to work out—just because he wanted to watch them feel the pain that he knew he felt the first time he did the same workout.

Goggins shared on the podcast that he used to want everyone to have pain, but now he's transcended that. At some point, the pain of other people stopped mattering to him and now, the only pain that mattered to him was his pain. This resonated with Michael at very ethereal level.

Goggins said: "It's when you feel the pain that is the point at which you decide who you are going to be." Are you are going to be the person that quits when the pain is there or you are going to be the person that knows "it's just pain" and keep going, to putting everything that you have into finishing what you started and leaving everything right there?

What he said changed how I looked at pain and my desire to push through it.

Right now, it's your job to find out what your area of expertise is and what makes you an authority. Then, it's your job to find out what pain your ICP is experiencing and what they need to do to push through it. From there, match your authority and problem-solving strategies with their problems.

When you write your content, you want to hit your consumer between the eyes. You want to know what keeps them up at night and what they desire in making that go away. Once you do that, you want to craft a story. Stories and messaging to the right person are hugely impactful and once you put them in a book, they become an irresistible offer to those who view you as being an authority.

As you provide more and more content to your audience, the more they trust you and the more content they want to consume. The more they consume, the more they trust you, the more they want to stay around, buy from, and tell people about you.

Writing a book and establishing authority to build an audience that will eventually become an army of loyal followers is the absolute recipe for success in helping you build your Life by Strategy.

DIGITALPRESIDENT.COM/COMMUNITY

CHAPTER 8

YOUR MILLION PERSON SALESFORCE

"Even though it is pretty easy to create a book these days, people will assign significant authority to you if you have a book and a media 'ecosystem.'"

—Dan Kennedy

We were selling a book almost every minute. Initially, we thought some type of weird computer hack was filling out order forms online. At first glance, we were virtually sure of it, but we needed to confirm our suspicions. We opened one of the confirmation receipts and it showed one person had purchased two copies. We checked the next receipt and we saw what we thought was a similar mistake. We even saw that one person purchased three copies. As we scrolled through the purchases, though, we realized that none of it was a mistake.

We were selling books and it was everything we thought it would be.

All of this being said, the concept of selling a book to build a business had actually never crossed Michael's mind. Well that is not actually true; it had crossed his mind because recently, he found some of the notes he took after spending a day in the basement with Dan Kennedy, where he had written down, "A book is just like a well-written sales letter."

Almost four years before that on a video, Jay Abraham had shared his philosophy on why a person should consider writing a book. He had watched the video several times, but for some reason he never "heard" what Abraham was saying. In the video, Abraham shared a concept on gifting books, and the positioning it gave you in the marketplace. Seeing these notes and watching these videos, Michael, still today, can't believe he missed this brilliant concept that was sitting right in front of his eyes, almost daily.

With the internet—and audio books—the consumption of a person's message had the chance to grow exponentially. Like everything after writing his sixth book, Michael finally understood why and how a book that was done right could help launch a business by giving potential clients an ideal path to consume a message—a message where one could address their skepticisms, create a bond, demonstrate proof, and actually show them samples—a message of how one could help them go from where they were to where they wanted to be.

And we had to look no further than our own book for proof.

In December 2016, a client of ours from the southwestern part of Missouri—about 425 miles from where we are in Texas—made a five-figure investment in our inside sales agent boot camp on a Sunday, then got in her car and drove most of that day so she could attend the event, which started on Monday.

The client's name is Carolyn and she purchased our book only six days prior. She read it cover to cover and went through the accompanying training we provided online in those six short days.

After going through the book and the training, Carolyn called to inquire about our boot camp and Michael took her call. The striking thing about the sales call is that Michael didn't really need to do a whole lot of selling.

He simply had a conversation with her.

And to that point, the conversation was just that: a conversation. There was no hard selling or hard closing on the call. In fact, some of the things they were talking about Michael had forgotten were in the book.

Within five minutes of talking with Carolyn, Michael realized that she already knew the story. She already had a good grasp of the who, what, when, where, how, and why that you normally cover on sales calls and she was ready to make a purchase after simply getting a few questions answered.

The book had already done the job of selling Carolyn on us, our Core Philosophy, and what we could do to help her.

In the end, she pretty much knew everything she needed to make a decision prior to calling, she just needed to get clear on a couple of things, all of which were to be covered in our upcoming boot camp.

The call took a total of 15 minutes, and you already know what happened next.

How, you might be asking yourself, could a book have influenced someone at such a high level to make them plunk down $12,500 after a short phone call and then spend the rest of their weekend driving to attend a four-day event in another state?

The answer is simple: Your book is your highest leverage point. It's your million-person sales force that works without your direct efforts to convert suspects to prospects so that you can convert the prospects to high-paying clients.

It wasn't just any book though … it was our book, the one we wrote about how we started a company from scratch leveraging nothing but the predictive data of our perfect ICP for one of the biggest transactions a person could make in their life.

And through consumption of our book, she was able to move from awareness, consideration, and then to a buying decision. She also had all of her skepticism addressed, leading her to suspended any disbelief she was experiencing so she could make a decision that would move her closer to her goals and desires.

The book was great because it actually solved a real problem in a marketplace. A great book nails one of the key components of great marketing: "Message To Market Match." Our book helped people get customers, even if they did not have any money to advertise, and more importantly, it gave them a real competitive advantage in their marketplace.

In a "noisy niche," we created a way to position ourselves so differently that people will drop everything they're doing to drive hundreds of miles to become a client.

These are the kind of results you get when you nail your book.

As you saw, it was the key ingredient in getting Carolyn to make a five-figure investment and then spend about a week out of her business, away from home, on 48-hours' notice.

It was also the catalyst to help us build—and agents of clients to do the same thing—fast. It wasn't just any audience, it was one that shared the Core Desire that we knew we could enthusiastically help them achieve.

What's even better is that many of the agents' clients who attended boot camp after getting and reading the book are now paying as much as $2,300 per month for us to provide solutions where many of them are making $50,000 or more per month.

And it all started as a result of them successfully implementing and executing the strategies in our book.

You see, writing a book with the strategic intent of adding value to a defined client (your ICP) and target market with a very clear solution and articulated value proposition gives you a platform to attract a client with relative ease.

It also helps you generate all the raw material you need to create a sales and marketing funnel to automate your messaging and consumption to move your Ideal Client through the process of delivering to them their desired outcome—making them a raving fan who's willing to invest in you and your product or service.

Lastly, it positions you as a legitimate authority in your space, which will have an exponential impact on all your sales and marketing efforts.

Here's an example of how impactful writing a book can be: In 2006, Michael Schultz, principal of the Wellesley Hills Group, of Framingham, Mass.—a marketing consultancy for professional service providers—said: "The vast majority of the authors we surveyed—96 percent—said they did realize a significant positive impact on their businesses from writing a book and would recommend the practice."

He maintained that the main benefits of writing the book are indirect. Specifically, even the authors whose books were great sellers didn't derive a significant amount of income from book sales. The benefits they mentioned were best related to "generating more leads, closing more deals, charging higher fees, and getting better speaking engagements."

We've certainly experienced this in our own businesses.

What you'll find is writing a book lets you fight for, and hold onto, the mindshare of your clients: something that you must do if you're going to maintain long-term, profitable relationships with them.

It's the gateway to all your content creation and delivery as well as everything you want to do in growing your business as big and wide as you want.

Clarity Is the Name of the Game

Since you started your business, you've been likely providing products and/or services to your clients without really thinking clearly about 1) what your brand really stands for in the eyes of your consumer, 2) how your client wants to be communicated to, and 3) what your customer's journey looks like from beginning to end.

This isn't necessarily a bad thing, as you can experience a modicum of success by doing what Zig Ziglar identifies as finding needs and filling them and finding problems and solving them without that level of clarity.

That said, if you're looking to design a Life by Strategy and create an automatic pipeline of raving, long-term fans, you really need to get clear on all three aspects of your business—especially from the POV of your ICP.

What's exciting is that the process of writing your book is going to get you clear—crystal clear—on everything you need to say and do to attract your ICP to you and retain them as a member in your legion of fans.

The process starts with you first understanding that you're looking to teach the principles you know to your ICP and show them how to apply these principles to their specific situation in solving their problem(s).

The reason you need to adopt this mindset is because up until now, you have just done what you do without thinking about how it's done or explaining to someone how it's done. It's like former NFL coach Bill Parcells put it: "Spare me the labor, just give me the baby." Your clients don't want a song and dance, they just want your product as part of the transaction.

But you don't want just transactions, you want relationships. And to create the strongest ones, you must teach and explain what you do and how you do it so your clients want more of it and you.

You must deconstruct your expertise and help your clients understand not just the expertise itself, but the inner workings behind how and why it works. You're looking to communicate what you know to someone else in such a way that they can grasp it and put it to work themselves in their own business.

You also need to be able to communicate why things work the way they do and you want to do it in a way that's easy to grasp. The best salespeople are able to clearly, concisely communicate mental models (thought processes people use to make decisions) to help people make decisions faster and remove complexity from the thought process.

You don't want to come across as if you're just randomly nailing boards together hoping to come up with a solution. Readers need you to connect the dots for them. Giving the reasons how things work is great, but you want your readers—your ICPs—to be able to say to themselves: "I'm having these problems, you have the solutions, and I know why they're going to work for me."

When you can make that happen, you have truly delivered what your clients want and you've made yourself the number-one choice in their mind to help them meet their needs. And that's what this whole process is all about.

Now, you may be thinking you're giving away the "goose that lays the golden eggs," but it's the sharing and inner workings of your expertise that will get your ICP to want to find out even more from you and have you solve their problems for them instead of doing it themselves.

Keynote speaker and author Erika Andersen states that "people have often been surprised when I've said this—they question whether it's really a good idea to put your ideas out in public for anyone to see (and, by implication, steal). But our experience has been that the ideas in a book quite often whet people's appetite for more in-depth knowledge or consulting."

Only after you've adopted that frame of mind are you able to move on to the next part of the process: Brainstorm all the situations that your ICP is facing that are causing them pain or preventing them from reaching their goals, and then determine all of the solutions to their problems.

As part of the process, you'll also want to identify all their dreams, wants, and desires and any objections to buying your product and/or service as a means to making those dreams come true.

You can't just know what they want; you need to know what their fears and skepticisms are and what things they just don't want or like as it pertains to any solution you would provide to them.

When you take this deep dive into understanding your clients and what goes into guiding their decisions, it becomes easy to create a framework to communicate with them. You now have a tremendous amount of power in all your marketing and sales efforts to influence people and to interact with them on every level.

In going through this process and writing a book, you also have brand clarity.

According to Erika Andersen, brand clarity is defined as: "Having a book or books that lay out the key intellectual property or the core models or principles of your business [that] really helps potential clients understand what you're about and how you can be valuable to them."

It will be so clear that you'll even be able to come up with the title of your book, webinar, blog, and other materials with ease.

Lastly, you also have all the content and information you need to tell your Core Story (and sub-stories) that are going to resonate with people and attract them so they and you are aligned to achieve a desired outcome. By distilling down your expertise into fundamental principles that people can latch onto, you have everything you need to get your book out of your head and into print.

But you must do the work first and go through the process of knowing every possible scenario your ICP could and would encounter in working with you. Otherwise, the process simply does not work.

All Roads Lead to Your Book

Prior to the advent of the internet, we would find out about a book by seeing something on television, getting an advertisement in the mail, having it recommended by a friend, learning about it at a seminar, or seeing it at the library or bookstore.

There were no blogs, web videos, emails, or texts to give us snippets from the book or opinions and information from the author. Consumption was harder to foster in that environment and it cost a lot of money to get in front of consumers to make the pitch as to why they should buy your book.

And, although you had authority with people because you were an author, it was hard to cement your legacy and leverage your authority into ancillary money-making strategies. Experts who got to speak in front of others had to do a tremendous amount of legwork and spend thousands of hours making inroads into their respective communities.

Today, you are able to establish authority and grow your client pool and revenue quickly by leveraging not only your book, but also all of the other marketing and communication platforms that are available to you today on the internet. Most importantly, though, you are driving the entire consumption process and ensuring that a large number of people read your book, which then allows you to control the narrative with them and maximize your results.

TOFU, MOFU, BOFU

There is no shortage of means by which you will be able to reach and influence your prospects and clients: book, blog(s), Facebook, Twitter, emails, texts, videos, webinars, teleseminars, websites, and even direct mail.

Each of these strategies has its own unique set of powers and can be used by you to bring people aboard the Customer Journey with you. As part of your overall strategy, you will use your book to create the content and material for all of the marketing and communication done through these various technologies.

Your goal is to use them in various stages of your funnel to ensure that at some point during your prospect's and client's interactions with you that they end up purchasing and then reading your book:

Top of Funnel (TOFU) – This is the point at which your folks get involved with you. When we wrote *Inside Sales Predictability*, Woods had to leverage the book in a way that allowed us to get an unfair advantage with our marketing budget. He did by making the book a Universal Offer. A Universal Offer is something of value with a wide enough appeal that you "offer" to prospects in exchange for their contact information (usually email address). The Universal Offer is usually low cost or no cost and it gives interested prospects a way to find out more about you and even help them solve some problems they are having.

Getting people interested need not necessarily translate into an allowable customer acquisition cost. One thing we did right was pick our target market: Inside sales is a huge buzz phrase in our industry because most clients who get their clients online don't want to prospect. Woods believed that offering a book that spoke to how agents could replace themselves on the phone would be a huge hit. He was right, as we sold thousands of them in less than six months.

We also included scripts and dialogues for prospecting and videos from our live boot camp for anyone who purchased the book. We moved the Free Line way, way back on this offer so that it was an absolute no-brainer for people to buy our book and take us up on our offer.

Remember, your book is your best salesperson. It does all the storytelling and it connects all the dots so that the Carolyns in your world show up ready to make an investment in what you have to offer in helping them solve their biggest problems.

You're not required to use a book at TOFU, but it is a huge point of attraction to give something of value away that gets folks hooked on you and what you do.

Middle of Funnel (MOFU) – At this point, you're looking to move people along in the process and get them to internalize even more of your material. They've gotten involved with you and it's time to talk with them—webinar or teleseminar—and really share your expertise so that they can start taking what you know and using it to help themselves.

With the book written and our Core Philosophy and teaching points well thought out and in print, we were able to create a kick-butt webinar that had all of the talking points and sales elements nailed. What we talked about in the webinar came directly from the book. We didn't need to think about what we were going to put in the webinar because it was already done for us. This shortened our creation and delivery time to the market.

We were also able to create Facebook posts, emails, and videos to drive people to the webinar as well as to TOFU. Again, all of it came from what we wrote in the book. The process was seamless and easy to implement, and it grew our marketing efforts geometrically.

Also, when people signed up for the webinar, they received emails and texts that had signature lines that drove them to a website where they could find out more about the book.

Bottom of Funnel (BOFU) – At this point, you want ready, willing, and able buyers to come out of BOFU. Not only are you using content from your book, you're also leveraging any testimonials from successes you've had with others who have worked their way through the process. You want these people to sing your praises and validate your expertise whenever possible.

At this stage—and at all stages for that matter—you will have content from your book that continues to 1) move your prospects and clients to the natural conclusion that working with you is the right choice, and 2) to buy your book and read it so you can control the sales and consumption process.

If you're like us, you interact with a lot of people every day and many of them are coming to you looking for guidance on how to solve problems. There are lots of things you could do to get them to their desired conclusion, but telling them to go pick up a specific book (even giving them that book) and read it is the best thing you can do for them.

Yes, you can tell them to check out a website, go see someone speak, hop on a webinar, read a blog, etc., and by all means, do that—it's not bad advice. At the end of the day, though, if you want them to get the advice and direction they need to resolve the issues they are having, you tell them to read the best book for their situation.

Hands down.

Your book is the lowest barrier of entry to get access to you and your expertise. There's a small investment, the book can be purchased anywhere at any time, and it's only a matter of days (even hours) before someone can have access to you and what you're all about. As well, they can find out about your book from any number of elements within your marketing funnel in a matter of minutes after being introduced to you.

Your book also opens the gateway to speaking engagements, webinars, teleseminars, boot camps, podcasts, and other platforms to tell your story. Your content for each of these is driven by your book and the possibilities are limitless.

Finding out about you, your book, and what you do has never been faster or easier than it is in today's technological environment.

Once someone finds you and your book, they can refer you to other people very easily. You see, books are like batons: They can get passed easily between people to transfer both excitement and knowledge about a particular person or topic. Your goal is to write a book and create amazing content that makes people not only want to consume it, but also want to share your book with the people in their lives.

When you do this, you will have created your million-person sales force. You'll have people sharing your story and expertise, and then either recommending or sharing your book with them. Your properly written and executed book and marketing funnel will do the rest of the work for you.

Taking Charge of Your Book's Consumption

If you write a book, get it published, and put it on Amazon, you'll likely sell a few copies. While this is a strategy to get books sold, it's not really a great strategy to drive the consumption of your book that is aligned with creating your Life by Strategy.

To accomplish your goals, you want to drive consumption while building a list of buyers who have received the clearest articulation of your value proposition. And what we mean by that is this: Your book is going to attract the right clients—your ICP, if you will.

When you attract your ICP and communicate your Core Philosophy in a way that resonates with them, you want to communicate to them your Core Philosophy, as we talked about in earlier chapters.

The reason you want to build a list of buyers is that you always want to have people lined up to consume your book when they are ready. You see, your book might not hit someone over the head the first time they read it. For that matter, they might not read it at all the first time it's in their hands.

Michael got a copy of Napoleon Hill's *Think and Grow Rich* when he was a much younger man, but it sat on his shelf for years. Several years after getting the book, he finally read it, and it changed his life. Like Michael, some readers may only consume your book and take action when they are ready, hence the adage: "When the student is ready, the teacher will appear."

The good news for you, though, is that you have many advantages that Napoleon Hill didn't have. You have multiple outlets in the form of blogs, emails, texts, videos, etc., to continue to incubate the buyers on your list. As a result of this, you will have multiple opportunities to influence your prospects and clients until they are ready to make a move. And when they are, your book will be there to move them along to the next phase of their journey.

For instance, a prospect, current client, or even a past client could read your book and continue consuming your materials—even be in alignment with your Core Philosophy and believe in you and what you do—and not make a purchase or do business with you for an extended period of time. Then one day, they see or hear something from you on one of your platforms and take action after doing that.

We experienced this in our own business.

We had someone from Austin, TX that had been on our list for several years. He'd consumed tons and tons of our content in the form of emails, sales pages, webinars, and teleseminars, and up until last November, he had made zero purchases with us.

In November, he purchased our book and after reading it, made the decision to invest in our inside sales agent boot camp. Since attending boot camp, he's committed to an investment of almost $30,000 with us over the next 12 months.

That's an investment of over $42,000 in one year after not spending a dime on anything with us in the prior several years—all after reading our book.

Imagine how awesome it would be to get a sizeable, five-figure investment from a client who has either been dormant for a while or has been following you and never made a purchase.

Incredible!

The more strategic you are in designing your communication with your ICP, the better job you do deconstructing your expertise for consumption by your ICP, the more you understand your ICP's situation and solutions to their obstacles, bottlenecks, constraints, and desired outcomes, the better job you do of laying out your book in a linear fashion and explaining the "why" behind what you do, the better results you are going to have in not just getting your book sold, but also in building your audience of consistent consumers for your business.

Please remember, outstanding results come from being strategic in doing all of these things when writing your book. Winging it or guessing just won't get the job done.

If you're like many people, you don't think that you have enough information to write about. The good news is that as you deconstruct what you know into specific points and principles, you'll find that you have a lot to talk about.

In addition, stories will come out during the process and that will help make what you're teaching become entertainment, a key element in making sure people read your book cover to cover. You'll want to talk about your successes and failures and the gains and pains you experienced along the way. The more stories you can tell and the more you can connect on an emotional level with your reader, the more people will read your book.

Writing a book helps you organize all your content and gets you extremely clear on all your branding, positioning, value proposition, ICP, and even your offer. As well, it really makes you think about your business and what you can do for people from their perspective. Plus, it helps you establish yourself as the go-to person for your industry or niche.

As you write your book, you're creating content that you can use as content for the other platforms you're going to create to expand awareness of your brand. Those technologies will not only help you get in front of more people, they'll also help you refer people back to your book so they can buy it and let it do the selling as they consume your expertise and stories.

Lastly, it's one thing to be an expert and to know how to solve people's problems. It's something altogether different to be able to show people how you do it in a way that they can easily wrap their head around so they can do it for themselves.

The byproduct of being able to do this isn't them wanting to do it all for themselves, it's them seeking you out to do it for them.

See **How To Write a Book That Makes Money Fast** at
digitalpresident.com/resources

CHAPTER 9

BUILDING YOUR AUDIENCE (Be Shirt Worthy)

"Win the crowd, win your freedom."

—Proximo, *The Gladiator*

What would you do if you lost 100 percent of your revenue overnight? Would you be able to survive and replace it in a short period of time (90 days or less), or would you have to close the doors to your business for good?

For most it's a scary thought to entertain, but for us, it was a reality. What we learned was having an audience with which you can communicate and depend upon can have a huge impact on whether or not your company would make it through such a catastrophic event.

Michael's journey of selling actual products and services online started in mid-2005. He and a friend had shared great success in real estate sales. In building their successful real estate businesses, they had also built relationships with hundreds of agents who were also friends and people with whom they shared solutions and learned about handling the different challenges agents face when growing their business.

This was the genesis of the huge audience he built with his real estate consulting business. He had gotten so good at generating clients constantly online, people would simply buy anything he told them to.

At that time, Michael learned about a very innovative technology that used video to greet new visitors to a website. This video could be placed on any website, and it was the very first affiliate revenue generating endeavor in which he had gotten involved.

That opportunity led to a joint venture partner with another company whose product worked along with the video subscription service like peanut butter and jelly on white bread. It was an exciting time because Michael's business and audience were growing at breakneck speed due to the fact that there was an exceptional amount of demand in the marketplace for what he was selling.

Part of what led to his success was the fact that he had unknowingly been building a very loyal audience. From day one, he started collecting business cards and contact information from every agent he met, whether or not they were in his marketplace, at a conference he was attending, or just speaking with him on the phone. He had already met or been in contact with thousands of real estate agents prior to starting his business.

At the same time, he was also using the technology of now-CRM giant, Salesforce, to house, service and grow his database. It had only become a public company a couple of years earlier, but he saw it as a necessary tool for him to get from where he was to where he wanted to go in building a responsive group of people to whom he could sell. One of the bonuses for him was that Salesforce had the contact information for thousands of real estate agents, which provided to him a ready-made pool of prospects to align with and sell to.

With the website and this video technology that was only available through Michael's company, agents couldn't get enough of his product. Plus, with an incentive program that gave website owners theirs for free when they referred four people who bought, he was bringing on a hundred-plus new customers every month.

In an effort to create more value, he started doing bi-weekly training calls. As well, he was producing and distributing content left and right. At one point, he was spending $5,000 a month outsourcing article creation.

Michael enjoyed a tremendous amount of success from providing these calls for a couple of reasons:

1. The calls were live trainings with a significant amount of Q&A that allowed for a high level of engagement between him and his clients. It was the perfect forum for him to deposit value while educating and entertaining his audience at the same time. Engagement and ongoing conversations that deposit value are key elements of creating a strong audience.
2. He brought a lot of strategies, systems, beliefs, and philosophies to the calls from outside the industry. Not only was the content unique and helpful, but it was also extremely thought provoking, which had his callers wanting to come back for more. In order to build your audience with some staying power, you must provide thought-provoking content that keeps your audience members engaged, wanting even more material and information from you.

3. The stuff he was sharing with people came directly from his own experiences in the real estate business. He was fighting the same daily battle they were, so he was able to connect with them on many levels and they could feel the passion he had for what he did. Your audience must be able to connect with, and feel, your passion for what you do if it is to be effective in helping you grow your business.

His content wasn't always planned out and ready to roll for each call, as sometimes he decided what he was going to talk about only minutes before the call. In the end, he delivered mad value at a very high level and as a result, his audience hungrily soaked in everything he shared with them.

Does this mean we don't want you to plan out your content strategy? In short, no. We absolutely do, and your book is *the* key element in all of that coming together. That said, it doesn't have to be perfect in the beginning. This is a process and not an event, and you can add a lot of value to your audience simply by sharing what you know and how it can help them in an open format like a Q&A.

Things were going incredibly well for Michael's company and it had actually reached 1,000 clients. In less than two years, he grew his company to over half a million in revenues, hired a small number of employees, leased some professional office space, and was planning to make a "ding" in the planet as he staked his claim as a successful entrepreneur who was making a change in people's lives.

And then it was gone.

As you remember, the real estate market shifted dramatically in a very negative direction. The website he was selling literally disappeared, which meant the other technology he was selling needed to find other industries to sell to in order to keep its own head above water. It appeared that he was dead in the water with nothing to generate revenue for his company.

To make matters worse, he was only a couple of weeks away from having his first annual event where he made a $50,000 commitment at a major venue for rooms, food, audio/visual equipment, and staff support.

It was a little unsettling, to say the least. He needed to find a solution and he needed to find it fast.

After brainstorming like mad, Michael came to the realization that although he didn't have his bread-and-butter product to sell anymore, he had a group of people with whom he had built a relationship over the last couple of years. These people were the agents whom he was coaching and with whom he had built a tremendous amount of trust and recognition.

In essence, he had an audience and he had their attention, which means he had a legitimate opportunity to not just survive, but thrive, after what could have likely been the death knell for his business. So, he did the only thing he could do: he marketed new products and services to his audience via email, text, and the internet.

At this point, Michael had transcended being an agent: He was on his path to becoming a world-class internet marketer.

As you remember from Chapter 6, Michael launched a continuity program called Inner Circle, the same program that scored 255 "cha-chings" in twenty-four hours and almost killed Michael's phone. At the same time, he also launched a listing lead service as well as his agent coaching business … all to the same group of people.

The result was incredible.

Not only did he replace the lost revenue, he more than doubled it. Within 90 days of having *all* of the income sucked down the drain, he replaced it with almost $85,000 of recurring revenue per month.

The important thing to note here is that he had never charged them directly for anything prior to doing this. They paid their money directly to the two companies whose products he sold, but never to him.

Of course, in the prior couple of years, he tried to do a couple of webinars, and even some teleseminars, through email blast invitations for this group of people in order to generate some additional income online. Overall, however, he had no internet marketing or marketing funnel experience—and no significant revenue from our earlier efforts—to speak of when he started marketing his own products to his audience. Plus, at the time, he had no real strategy for creating, implementing, and monetizing anything they were doing.

'Essentially, they failed at that aspect of their business. But they did have an audience and most certainly had their attention. Their list wasn't huge, but it was big enough for them to make some inroads.

'Michael went from a list of 300 enthusiasts in 2006 to having as many as 1,500 people who purchased something from him by the end of 2008, all through sheer grit and determination in selling websites. As well, he built a list of 30,000 subscribers who opened his emails and consumed his content. When he transitioned his business to an internet marketing model, he still had about a thousand engaged people who were actual clients in his audience with around 14,000 subscribers on his email list. What he had was an audience that he could leverage to grow his business long into the future.

Understanding Audience

Before we proceed any further, it's important to discuss what an audience is and how powerful it is in building your business. Your audience is comprised of real human beings that:

- Consume your material one time, but return intentionally at a later date to read your content
- Seek, in earnest, to consume new content you provide
- Regularly sign up to get your content from a "push" system (e.g. They join your mailing list where you have control over what you send and when you send it to them.)

As soon as you are able to, you want members of your audience to sign up for email consumption of your material because it shows that they are more committed to getting and reading your content. More importantly, as you deliver even more high-value, life-changing content through your emails to them, the more allegiance you earn from them as they anxiously await each piece of content you disseminate. Lastly, as they stay with you over a period of time and establish a relationship with you, they will be open to a mutually beneficial situation when you have something to sell to them.

To create this relationship and give it staying power, you want your audience to share a Core Identity—a sameness that's rooted in what the essence of your brand is about. We see this in music all the time—as in Chapter 7 with Michael and Kriss Kross—when famous musicians have true fans that want to dress just like them. It's the feeling of: "I can be like them if I wear the same clothing." The best is when it happens around a brand that has meaning to them and that they feel represents them and their beliefs.

Two of our favorite core identities with our audience are being a Hit Maker or Hitman. Our core audience are winners who we help win bigger and faster—to create hits—simply by giving them the road map. At their core, they are dangerous, like a gun. Whatever you point them at, they kill.

They kill their goals and they make their problems disappear. They get the job done. What we represent is a small group of super-elite people who are behind the scenes making hits.

Take the music industry, for instance. Jimmy Iovine, the mastermind behind Beats headphones, and Dr. Dre, the genius behind the hip hop industry's biggest albums: They make hits, but they're also behind some of the elite people who kill it in the music industry, too.

We love Dr. Dre's music. It's amazing, but we also love Randy Travis. Randy Travis makes hits as well. There are lots of famous musicians that make hits. In our eyes, it could be any famous musician. It's not about the music you like, though, it's the appreciation for the music—for the hit itself.

In the music industry—and in any other industry for that matter—we recognize a hit: from the packaging to the quality content they create consistently, from the onboarding to everything in between. We see when someone puts in the work. They get the job done, make hits, and get big numbers.

When you can do this, you can attract and build a list of subscribers that can help you be uber successful in building your business and creating a Life by Strategy. It's worth mentioning here that having as few as 1,000 diehard supporters—folks who will buy everything you sell, drive hundreds of miles to come and see you, and consume every smidgen of content you produce—is great benchmark for you to hit.

You see, with just 1,000 raving fans, you can make $100,000 by scoring a scant $100 profit off of each one of them from sales of a single product. Do that once a quarter for a year, and you're looking at $400,000 in profit without anyone having to break the bank to buy from you. That's not a bad sum of money for staying connected to, and influencing, a relatively small core group of people who dig you at a very deep level.

Having 1,000 customers is a reasonable goal to aim for and a lot easier to get than a million fans. Millions of fans willing to lay out their hard-earned cash is exciting, but it's not a realistic outcome to try to attain, especially when you are in the beginning stage of growing your business and list of subscribers. But 1,000 enthusiasts is a number you can make happen.

See **The Fastest Way to Build An Audience of People that are Most Likely to Buy** at digitalpresident.com/resources

Ideally, you might actually be able to remember the names of a thousand people. Heck, if you added only one new legit fan daily, you could gain a thousand in less than three years.

Keep this in mind: 1,000 is not the hard and fast rule. The specific number you need to shoot for is based on your metrics and business. If you earn $50 per year per true fan, then you need 2,000. The same thing goes if you can make $200 per year, as you'll need only 500 true fans.

At the same time, your Life by Strategy may dictate that you only need $75,000 per year to live on, so you would make a downward adjustment in your numbers. If you're in a relationship with someone who owns the company with you or if you have a partner, then you need to double the number of fans to hit the income target. If there are multiple people involved, you'll need to multiply by more.

You get the math here.

If you would like, you can calculate the value of a true fan by aiming to get a single day's wages a year from them. Can you add enough value, and entertain your fans sufficiently enough, to earn one day's labor? It's a stretch goal, but not out of the realm of 1,000 people around the world.

Certainly, there's nothing saying you can't grow a bigger audience. If you want to be a rock star, then more power to you. We just wanted you to know there's serious power in 1,000 subscribers and that group of 1,000 people needs to be passed on the way to one million.

Consistency in your message and in the delivery of content will ultimately foster the trust you'll need to get the members of your audience to respond not only with a hunger for more content, but also with their checkbooks.

You'll know that your audience is dialed in to your message when they are wearing your brand and your message on the shirts on their backs, helping you build your audience themselves.

May We Have Your Attention, Please?

To help you create your Life by Strategy, you too will need a highly responsive audience. To create this community of active subscribers, you must first get the attention of your ICP and then keep it.

You'll keep their attention by providing consistent content for them to consume, which allows you to strengthen your relationship with them with each new piece of material you provide.

Having an attentive, involved, and responsive audience not only helped us save our bacon, it was the launching point to us growing our business into what it is today, a company that generates over 8 million dollars per year with an audience of over 200,000 people, and growing.

In order to build a tribe of highly responsive subscribers, you need to first capture people's attention. And while it's said that there's no such thing as bad publicity, we recommend that you do everything you can to get people's attention in as positive a way as possible.

In order to command attention, you need to find your voice. Your voice is your unique style and way of saying things. It's driven by who you are, authentically, and by your audience. It's your point of view and it needs to resonate with your audience. Before you put pen to paper, so to speak, you must decide what your voice is going to be, and you absolutely must know to whom you're speaking: your ICP.

In several places in prior chapters, we've tried to hammer home the importance of nailing who your ICP is. The more you know about them: pains, gains, goals, etc., the easier it is going to be to get—and keep—their attention. You're going to be talking to your ICP across all channels using this voice, so it's crucial that you keep your ICP in mind in all the content you create. The good news is that your content is largely derived from what's in your book, so this shouldn't be a Herculean challenge.

As part of finding your voice, you're going to want to use words, phrases, and ideas that are specific to you. To a certain extent, it will be like creating your own language with a unique tone of voice, jargon, and speech patterns that identify you to the reader/listener. When you do this, two things will happen:

1. You'll pull in the folks that like you and are like you. Law 3 of the Six Principles of Influence by Dr. Robert Cialdini is "Like or Liking." People want to do business with those that they like or that they think are like them. You'll attract people because they're familiar with the type of language that you're using.

2. You'll repel people who either don't understand what you're talking about or are offended by what you're saying and how you're saying it. Folks who don't resonate with your Core Philosophy or your Core Beliefs and the way that you speak about them will be pushed away from you. This is a good thing because you're looking for followers and fans who want to hear from you.

It's been said: "If you don't stand for something, you'll fall for anything." Finding your voice helps you articulate clearly to people what you stand for so they can either be with you or driven away by you. When you master your voice and create this division between the two groups of people, you'll be employing the principle of polarization.

Polarization creates two distinct factions—people who are either with you or against you—and the lines are clearly drawn between the two groups based upon what you stand for. It's important because it makes your message very clear and easy to pick up for those who identify with you. The benefit of this is that people can easily align with your message and the passion surrounding it, while at the same time they can take that message and share it with other people clearly and effectively in helping you grow your audience.

Failing to be polarizing means that the message you are sharing will either be missed completely, attract the wrong people, attract everyone, or attract nobody. No matter what the outcome is in this case, none of them are good in helping you build a list of subscribers.

Think about celebrities like Kanye West, Kim Kardashian, Gwyneth Paltrow, and especially President Donald Trump. These people garner a tremendous amount of media attention and the public is either for them or against them. There is very little middle ground with any of these types of people. They are all extremely polarizing.

Let's look at what having a clear voice and position can do to attract and then influence an audience. Early on in the 2016 election, Trump had roughly a 30 percent chance of winning the presidency. He was having a hard time overcoming the apathy and complacency that had taken hold of the American public when it comes to government. Trump realized that he had to "stir the pot" and get people's emotions stoked.

He had to get them to be unhappy with the status quo and all that the Democratic Party stands for. He had to stand out in a way in which he would either get people's attention and influence them to be on his side, or repel them to want to support the other candidates ... and that's exactly what he did.

How did he do it? How did he become so polarizing? He used the Democratic Party and the status quo as a common enemy. All the naysayers, doubters, and those who contradicted him were thrown into this identity of "the enemy." From Trump's perspective, this enemy needed to be overcome—destroyed if you will—in order to "Make America Great Again."

He got people fired up over the damage that he believed had been done by the enemy and sent the message that not only shouldn't the American public not take it anymore, but also that they should elect him to make things better.

David Smith of *The Guardian* said this about how polarizing Trump is:

> Trump was wildly ill-disciplined. There was outrageous behavior and offensive statements that alienated women, African Americans, Mexicans, Muslims, disabled people and, ultimately, believers in constitutional democracy. In any normal year, such a volatile package would have been disqualifying. But while those voices were amplified in the media, there were plenty of people who agreed with him ... Trump was the ultimate protest vote with obvious echoes of Brexit. Film-maker Michael Moore told NBC's Meet the Press in October: "Across the Midwest, across the Rustbelt, I understand why a lot of people are angry. And they see Donald Trump as their human Molotov cocktail that they get to go into

the voting booth on November 8 and throw him into our political system. I think they love the idea of blowing up the system."

The enemy was there and Trump was going to be the "Molotov cocktail" that blew it up.

Trump wasn't trying to appease or appeal to everybody. He stood for what he stood for and he was grounded in his beliefs and his Core Philosophy: "Make America Great Again."

His message aligned with voters' desired outcomes and he was consistent and unabashed in delivering that message. People either loved him or hated him, and those that loved him would do anything to get him into office … and they did.

To Trump's credit, he had a huge audience before he started and it got bigger and bigger during the election. He was already known for making business great, being on television, publishing many books, real estate, golf courses, clothing, and using other slogans including "You're FIRED."

One of the things that made his message so effective and helped him be so productive in rallying his audience was his use of the media channel (the platform, if you will) from which he chose to do a lot of communicating: Twitter. He used this media tool to rally his audience and grow it exponentially. With just under 40 million followers, he is currently #21 out of the 380 million Twitter users who actively use the social media platform on a monthly basis. Regardless of your political beliefs, there's one thing Trump knows how to do: build a huge audience of raving fans.

During his campaign, he was completely unabashed in sharing his feelings on everything and anything: politics, sports, his competition, women, men, kids … it didn't matter. He took no crap from anyone and let his feelings be known, whether people wanted to hear them or not. His fans and subscribers wanted to hear what he had to say and relished in how strongly he voiced his opinions and beliefs on things.

He mastered getting their attention, nailed his message clearly and effectively, and spoke directly into the heart of the Core Identity of his subscribers. He was, and continues to be, a master at polarizing an audience.

You need to have the same mindset for yourself.

You want to make sure that you are not trying to appease or appeal to everybody. You really want to stand firm and be grounded in what your beliefs are and what your Core Philosophy is. The people that you want to attract and that are tuned into you are going to be even more drawn to you. They're going to be more trusting of you, especially if you are willing to sacrifice popularity in order to be grounded in what you believe.

It just makes them trust you more.

Jeb Bush's campaign and slogan were pretty much the antithesis to what Trump did. From the outset of his campaign, Bush's staff even had trouble with his campaign slogan. They used "Jeb can fix it," and "All in for Jeb," but those didn't exactly excite or inspire people to support and follow him.

By the end of his campaign, the slogan was reduced to a simple "Jeb!"

New Yorker columnist John Cassidy explained Bush's ineffectiveness to attract and gain followers in a very succinct manner: "In the end, they were reduced to going with 'Jeb!'. For movies, music albums, and books, a one-word title may suffice. For would-be Presidential candidates, it is a problem, especially if that word is the candidate's name, and the candidate is a bespectacled man just two years shy of retirement age."

Reading this, it should be no surprise to you that Trump won the Republican nomination for the presidency.

As you're creating attention, you want to engage with people. The world that we live in now, especially with social media, makes it easy to be social. Your ICP wants to have a two-way conversation with you. Virtually every social platform gives people a way to respond to content through comments, reactions, sharing, etc.

To engage people, you must bond with them. Bonding happens when your ICP reads/hears what you have to say and it resonates with them. To get and maintain that bond, you're going to want to tell stories and use metaphors.

Metaphors link the known with the unknown and make your content more interesting. Metaphors also help you create themes that cement your message in the mind and hearts of your readers and it makes it easier for them to consume your message.

As well, you'll want to write in a conversational tone to get and keep your reader engaged. If your ICP feels like you're engaging in a conversation with them in your content, they will be far more apt to continue to consume your content in an effort to keep the conversation going. Writing conversationally is more personal to the reader, which will help them identify more closely with you.

Lastly, to maintain people's attention and strengthen your bond with them, you'll want to acknowledge them and engage with them in conversation. Doing this will make them want to engage more deeply with you and your content. The more you engage them, the more they get pulled towards your narrative. The more they get pulled into your narrative, the more they feel like they are a part of what you are talking about. It's not just about being interesting to them, you must also be interested in them if you want their ongoing allegiance in you and your company.

When people start wearing the T-shirt, talking to you in your language, and commenting and engaging with you when you deliver content, they have given you their full attention.

Consumption Is the Name of the Game

As you start to gain your ICP's attention, your main goal is to get people to keep tuning back in. You don't want people to "watch your show once" and then never come back to watch it again.

The value exists in them becoming subscribers and then consuming your content—all of your content—on a consistent basis. You need to be dripping on them consistently across a variety of platforms so they can get a 360° appreciation for you, your product or service, and what you can do to help them.

Whatever you do, you need to be publishing in real time. If you think you should post, then post. Be omnipresent until you're the Incredible Hulk in a puddle. Like Trump, you need to pick the media platform that is going to be where your core audience hangs out and then be a content creation fiend. The goal is to get them to continue to pay attention by constantly depositing value and creating thought-provoking content.

If you're having some hesitation, don't worry, we all start with nothing. The most important thing you can do is to just start writing and posting content. If you've taken the time to understand your ICP and where they need help, then what comes out of your head onto the computer screen should be appreciated and consumed by your subscribers.

One of the best things you can do is learn how to craft your "stories with positive intent."

Providing regular content helps keep them stay engaged so you can deepen your relationship with your audience as they continue to consume more and more of your material. And, with the technology we have available today, you can deliver content anywhere in the world and then establish and strengthen your relationship with that person whether they live in Kalamazoo, MI or Kathmandu, Nepal.

As you recall, everybody in your audience is at a different stage in their process. Dan Kennedy always said the one thing he loved about writing books was that some of his best clients will tell him, "I bought that book two years ago or three years ago or five years ago." These are where his best clients come from—the people who pay him $34,000 to come visit him and spend time in his basement.

These are the people who've been hanging around.

Hanging around is consuming content and getting value to the point where your ICP has a big enough problem and that the exchange of the money that's required in order to get to the value is big enough that they're willing to write that check for $34,000 to go spend a day in the basement with you.

When people hang around, they are deepening their beliefs that you understand their problems more than they do. Therefore, you probably have solutions they have never even considered.

It's not just based in the value, it's also based upon them consuming the content over a period of time.

In Chapters 5 and 6, the Value Journey and Value Exchange and the respectively, we talked about the need to communicate properly with and provide value to your ICP based upon where they are in the process of getting to know you. The content you create and deliver is how you're going to communicate at each step along the way.

What this means is that each piece of content you deliver—email, text, blog post, video, etc.—needs to have a specific goal based upon each stage. You may have an introductory email that gets someone excited to click a link to check out a video of you introducing yourself. In that video, you may give a tremendous amount of value to your prospect in how you can help them solve a problem and then invite them to buy your book.

Once they purchase the book, there might be a link for the reader to go to a website to grab a document that they can use to further solve their problem. At that site, there may be an invite to a webinar where you can then sell your big product or even an introductory product.

The point here is that you must get people to consume your content to not only move them along the Customer Journey, but also to add value and build trust with them. The only way you can do this is by being strategic about what content you deliver and when you deliver it.

More importantly, the level of trust that you gain is going to be elastic to the amount of consumption of your content of your ICP. More content consumed, more trust. Less content consumed, less trust. It's really that simple.

In short, producing and distributing consistent content is the main element of driving consumption and building trust with your ICP, no matter where in the process they are in becoming a raving fan of yours.

Deliver Your Message with Congruency

We've been talking in various parts of this book about your Core Philosophy and how important it is to have it well developed before launching into writing your book. The reason we've recommended this is because it's going to be pervasive in the content you deliver to your consumers.

The message you choose to deliver must not only be delivered from day one of your ICP's indoctrination, it must also be delivered in every piece of content you deliver. There's a linear path your ICP must follow in order to go successfully go from not knowing you to wearing your shirt and looking to you as their Digital President. In order to get your ICP to the end zone, your message must be congruent with their wants, needs, and desires—as we discussed—especially, if you want to get and keep their attention.

Failing that, you risk losing your audience for good.

Here's a real-life example: Michael takes great care of himself and is always open to listening when someone approaches him with a product or strategy to be healthy. Recently, he was visited by someone who was involved in sports medicine and he was trying to get Michael to buy his service.

Unfortunately, the sales process didn't go well.

The challenge for this person was that his message and product weren't congruent with Michael's goals. There was no alignment whatsoever. Interestingly enough, the entire time that this person was talking, Michael kept saying to himself: "I should go hire a personal trainer and make a commitment to taking my fitness to the next level."

Suffice it to say that a sale wasn't made that day. The bad news for that person is that if he had connected with Michael, he likely could have closed the deal, because in Michael's mind there was a legitimate problem that needed solving.

It's a real-world situation that all businesses encounter and many business owners fail miserably at handling it properly. Succinctly put, if your product and message aren't congruent with what your ICP needs, you will completely miss the mark, no matter how great your product is and how much content you disseminate.

A word of caution here: While the process of creating and sharing your message in the right way is simple to execute, doing it improperly will cost you more than money—it could cost you your reputation and even your business. You're looking to attract the right people and repel the wrong ones. Getting this part wrong will repel virtually everyone and make it hard to get them back a second time around.

In Chapter 11, *Brand Power vs. Force*, we will help you get clear on your positioning and your message. Do not skip this chapter or step. We repeat: Do not skip this chapter or step! Nailing your brand and brand promise makes everything infinitely easier.

The last part of delivering your message effectively with congruency is repetition. People need to hear your Core Story more than once in order for you to reinforce your narrative and Core Philosophy with them. You need to tell your stories over and over and over again so that the message you are sending is received loud and clear. It's one part of the whole process that helps you resonate with your ICP.

How many times during Trump's presidential campaign did you hear the slogan—his Core Philosophy—"Make America Great Again"? More than you can count on 10 fingers and 10 toes, that's for sure! That wasn't done by accident; it was to ensure that Trump's Core Story and Philosophy were reinforced and internalized by all who heard it all the way up to voting day.

It's important you don't think that people aren't going to listen for a second, third, and fourth time simply because they've heard it before. To boot, there will always be someone who needs to hear it and hasn't, making repetition even more crucial.

Attracting People to Your Content

Charlie Gaudet, author and expert blogger, asks the question: "If you write an article online and no one reads it, does it make an impact?" His intent is tongue-and-cheek humor, but he brings up a great point. If people aren't attracted to your content, they're not going to read it. And if they don't read it, they're not going to find out about you or your product or service, which means you have no opportunity to get more content in front of them to build a relationship and trust.

In addition to the rules we've been championing thus far in the book—speaking your ICP's language, aligning your solution to a problem with your ICP's needs, making sure your Core Philosophy and Core Story are delivered through a consistent, congruent message, etc.—you must use some multi-channel marketing to attract even more people.

Using other methodologies that complement the standard strategies used to release content gives you the opportunity to appeal to consumers that you might otherwise not get in front of to introduce yourself and your product or service. For instance, you may have a podcast you created that you could bring to *Forbes* and have them release it to their audience, which has members that are foreign to you and what you do.

Here are some other off-the-beaten-path distribution channels that are excellent for attracting new subscribers to your fold:

- Facebook Sponsored Updates – Facebook allows you to run a post that is a sponsored ad/update from your company. It stands out as a professional element on their page and it's way more impactful and effective than a post on your page. It's a great way to get someone started on their Customer Journey with you. We use them regularly in our business.

- Online Press Releases – As you recall, third-party endorsements are huge influencers. Online press releases let the audience know you've done something special and there's something in it for them. Unlike their paper-driven predecessors, online press releases give you the opportunity to embed photos and videos. Research from Dan Zarella, social media scientist, indicates that this strategy can increase engagement by 55 percent for videos and 18 percent for images. You'll find that PRNewsWire, PRWeb, BusinessWire, and MarketWire are some of the more popular and effective online press release sites.

- Social Bookmarking – Storing and saving content and links on sites like Pinterest, Reddit, and Tumblr allow people to not only save your content for future/additional consumption, but they also allow for sharing, which is huge in helping you attract more people to see your content without your direct efforts.

- LinkedIn Sponsored Updates – Much like their Facebook counterparts, LinkedIn Sponsored updates provide unique, stand-out opportunities for people to see updates from your business, to consume content they might otherwise not have seen if you simply posted a link on your LinkedIn profile.

- Document Sharing Sites – These sites give you the opportunity to share slideshows, PDFs and webinars of your expert material. As well, these sites allow you to take some of your older, effective content and convert it for other media like blogs or slideshows. One such site, Slideshare, gives you the chance to put an entire PowerPoint slideshow on its site so people can consume it on their own time. The best part is that you can drive people to your website when they see your content on this site.

With a solid message that speaks to people's desires, you can attract a significant number of prospects to take part in your Customer Journey on the way to becoming a faithful, long-term subscriber.

Building a Community of Raving Fans

Everything we're sharing in this chapter boils down to helping you build a community of raving fans. As we mentioned earlier, you don't need to have an audience that's a million strong to enjoy success. Building to even a thousand can get you some amazing results in the shorter term and in building a much larger target audience of highly obedient fans.

Life and business success guru Tim Ferriss calls this strategy the "tip of the spear that leads to more." What that means is instead of trying to go build this huge audience, you really want to focus on your first thousand fans.

For example, when Mark Zuckerberg and his partners launched Facebook they started with college students, a very well-defined target audience. And, although Facebook wasn't rolled out to everyone all at once, it has grown to 1.94 billion active users. They touched a subset of a niche of people for their initial target audience and built trust with them. Once they did that, they had a platform and a foundation to build trust in their community to help it become the behemoth it is today.

The process of building your audience is generating content that will first perk up your ICP's ears to attract them your way. Then, as your audience grows, it becomes a throng of fans—raving fans—that become followers. These followers trust you and will do virtually whatever you ask them to do (legally, ethically, and morally). Once you have a trusted group of followers that communicates with you, and you, in turn, communicate back with them, you have a community.

The members of your community feel as if they have a strong relationship with you, and it deepens with each piece of content you distribute and every conversation you have with your followers. In the end, these members of your community feel like they are part of what you're doing and will likely stay with you for life, consuming your content and buying your products as you release them.

At this stage, you're no longer speaking "to" your audience, you are part of them and they are part of you. You're helping them reach their goals and through the law of reciprocity, they will now help you. They'll be an advocate for you. They'll embody your Core Philosophy and scream your battle cry along with you, just like Trump's followers did with "Make America Great Again."

At this stage, they will speak your language online and even defend you against people who try to tear you down. They aren't just part of your community, they're part of your ongoing conversation and even helping you create content around your platform.

When this happens, you and your business will forever be, "shirt worthy."

CHAPTER 10

THE COMMUNITY FUNNEL

———

"If you don't find a way to make money while you sleep, you will work until you die."

—Warren Buffett

In 2011, Michael took one of the biggest gambles of his business career and it almost ate his lunch.

In late summer of that year, as co-founder of one of the most prolific real estate coaching associations in the United States and Canada, he laid out $50,000 to hire one of the foremost consultants on business optimization as the keynote speaker at the first big conference he was hosting in the fall. As part of the program, he made a commitment for $500,000 to secure space at a luxury hotel just north of Dallas to host the event.

He also hired a video production company and spent a boatload of money on an elaborate video production (including renting a helicopter) for his online marketing efforts to build excitement about the event.

He even set up a private webinar for his prospects and clients to get live access to his keynote speaker, a guy who's been interviewed by Tony Robbins and is responsible for getting his clients over $9 billion in revenue from working with him.

Yes, that says *billion*.

It was the perfect plan and it had to be, because he was less than two months away from the event with few to no tickets sold or hotel rooms reserved.

What made it even tougher was folks were going to have to spend a few thousand bucks to come to the event and then be away from their family while they stayed at a hotel that charged $10 for a cup of coffee and $12 for a bag of chips.

It was going to be an amazing event that delivered a ton of value … but it wasn't going to be a cheap date.

As with all plans, things are subject to change and his situation was no exception.

Six weeks before the event, the filming went off without a hitch. The production team did an amazing job except for one thing: due to technical problems, there was virtually no video and absolutely no audio from their efforts.

Essentially, they recorded little, if any, usable material.

Michael was shocked and literally in disbelief, but he was a fighter and he figured out how to use what little video he had with some voiceovers to make it work.

Plus, he still had his webinar and people were lining up to get on it and hear what Michael's guest speaker had to say.

On the day of the event, over 4,000 people were registered and they were anxiously sitting by their computers for this once-in-a-lifetime opportunity to hear from a guy who charges $50,000 for one day of working with him.

Michael was fired up and he knew it was going to be a homerun.

And it was … for ten minutes … until the webinar crashed and nobody was able to see or hear anything.

To say the least, it was a monstrous debacle and it pissed off a lot of people, something you don't want to do when you're trying to get them to lay out a decent amount of cash to buy something from you.

At this point, he was roughly a month out from the event and he was still on the hook for a half a million dollars that he didn't necessarily have tucked under the mattress at home.

And still, he had almost no sales and reservations. He had to do something and he had to do it fast.

In taking stock of what he had to work with, he realized that he already had the ingredients for a funnel in place: a product that solved people's problems, an ICP, good contact information for his list of prospects, and most importantly, he had a book.

It wasn't Michael's book—it was the keynote speaker's book—but it was just as good because he was able to borrow his authority, expertise, and content to build trust and do everything he needed in creating and operating the funnel.

He used the book at the top of funnel as the Universal Offer, to engage with people to get their attention. It was a smashing success. So much so, in fact, that it crashed the server when we and our affiliates launched it to our collective audience.

As an aside, Woods was Michael's leading affiliate for the launch of that online marketing effort. He had a huge hand getting people to pick up the book and get on the webinar.

The launch was the most successful one he had ever done at the time, and the funnel produced enough sales opportunities to not only cover our nut, but also help Michael reach his goal of bringing in $1 million in revenue.

He was literally on the brink of disaster and the funnel—The Community Funnel— not only saved his bacon, but also it made the event hugely profitable.

What's even better is that many of the people who didn't buy a ticket to the actual event were still in his audience and ended up purchasing coaching or another product from him after the event was over. He's used that funnel with amazing success since then to sell tickets to his annual event for a $997 a seat at the very same hotel.

It has served him well, to say the least.

The Community Funnel vs. Other Funnels

A high converting sales funnel can truly change your business and your life. Imagine what your life would be like if you knew with absolute certainty that your funnel could automatically generate all the clients you'll ever need. It may seem like a dream come true, but that dream can become your reality if you're willing to put in the work.

The problem with a lot of the funnels out there today is that they are built solely on direct response marketing. Now, don't take that the wrong way, because we love direct response marketing. We've made millions of dollars with it, but relying on direct response marketing alone will not give you the kind of funnel that produces the long-term, consistent results you need to build your business and live your Life by Strategy.

Direct response marketing is designed to generate an immediate response from prospects and persuade them to take a particular action, such as opting into an email list, making a phone call to get more information, or purchasing something directly. Normally, there aren't many additional stages for the prospect to work through. As well, the goal usually isn't to move prospects down a path to where you can build a long-term relationship with them, it isn't to have them see you as the go-to authority in your niche, and it isn't for them to want to remain a loyal member of your community after they happily purchase your product or service.

With the Community Funnel, you're employing a leveraged content strategy. It provides helpful, relevant content at each stage of the Buyer Journey as your prospects move from the awareness stage to the consideration stage and then from there to the decision stage: specifically from TOFU to MOFU to BOFU and ultimately into a community.

As you know, a book helps you take a person from where they are to where they want to go. Your book will not only be your Universal Offer, but it will also give you all the content pieces you need in a linear format that you can easily align to the stages in your funnel. When you have a Community Funnel clearly communicating, educating, and demonstrating to your prospects that you can help them throughout their Buyer Journey, you'll build deep relationships, and your prospects will buy from you because they know, like, and trust you.

Other funnels only focus on the small group of immediate buyers. The Community Funnel converts immediate buyers, but it focuses on nurturing the majority of buyers that aren't ready to buy immediately. The Buyer Majority Principle states that only a small fraction of your prospects are ready to buy now. The majority of your buyers need to be nurtured over time until they're ready to become a client.

Other funnels' strategies don't add value, start conversations, and build relationships. The Community Funnel does. It creates subscribers that want your content on an ongoing basis, unlike most funnels that focus on a one-time bribe in exchange for a quick opt-in.

Additionally, other funnels may get your attention, but they likely won't keep your attention. They're not looking to create authority or build an audience. They're simply employing some carnival marketing strategies to get people to take immediate action.

Your market's attention is not free. Your book delivers a compelling message and gives you a strategy to get authority, positioning you to win before you start. Once you have authority, you enjoy the compound effect of getting attention and then having the ability to influence, which then leads to you be able to move your prospects down your funnel to the natural conclusion of them wanting to do business with you.

Most marketers don't create their funnels properly because they aren't listening to their prospects' needs, wants, and desires. As a result, their funnels don't get great results.

Listen to and understand your prospect's' situation: Where are they? Why are they there? Are they where they want to be? Once you know the answers to these questions, then communicate in a way that provides value, builds trust, and explains to them that you understand their problem better than they do. When you do this with a consistent message, you'll truly have your prospects' attention.

When it comes to constructing your funnel, you want to design your strategy around a relationship that you want to grow and nurture. Do not have a "win or go home" strategy. Don't build the funnel that repels people from wanting a long-term relationship with you. Rather, build the funnel that stays in touch with prospects and provides helpful, relevant content until they are ready to advance the relationship to the next stage.

Funnel: Not Just Another Buzz Word

Right now, you may not have an automated selling machine that makes money while you sleep, and since you're reading this book, you likely don't know where to start in building one.

Also, if you're like many business owners, you've tried a variety of marketing and list-building strategies, but you've never been able to put it all together in one comprehensive funnel. It's just a bunch of fragmented attempts at generating revenue that don't take your client through their buying journey automatically.

Now, this situation is neither good nor bad, it just means that you're not getting the results you want and deserve.

You might be in this predicament because you believe one of the following lies:
- I need fancy software to pull off a successful funnel.
- I need a big email list in order to have success.
- I have to spend a lot of money advertising to attract enough people.
- I'm not "techie" enough to build a funnel online.

The fact of the matter is that none of this is even remotely true. You can have—and will only need—a single, amazing funnel to accomplish everything you want to as long as you set it up properly.

A funnel is the path where your Buyer and Value Journey combine to provide your prospects with the consistent Value Exchange that moves them from not knowing you to loving you, from loving you to buying from you, and from buying from you to being a huge fan who stays in your community and sings your praises to your other followers.

Once you nail creating and implementing your funnel, you will be able to create clients, automatically, while you sleep. The marketing you do on the various platforms that are available to you—websites, social media, blogs, podcasts, video hosting sites, emails, texts, etc.—will continue to run automatically and do your selling for you 24 hours a day, 7 days a week.

Next to the book you write, your funnel will be one of your best salespeople because it will always be generating leads and sales for you, no matter what you're doing during the day.

As we've mentioned before, prospects will learn about you 1) at various stages of their journey to getting solutions to their problems, and 2) at some stage near the top of your funnel (which we will discuss in more detail shortly). Set up properly, your funnel will take them from that point and move them toward becoming a client.

And because of that, the funnel does the hard work so you don't have to.

As long as you think through the entire journey of taking someone from a cold prospect to a raving fan who is a member of your community, your funnel is all you'll need to generate consistent, recurring income.

Even More TOFU, MOFU, and BOFU

In the last chapter, we introduced you to the acronyms for Top of Funnel, Middle of Funnel, and Bottom of Funnel and gave you a cursory review of each section of the automated sales machine and how they work to produce paying customers.

In this chapter, we're going to dive deeper and talk about what elements of your content strategy you would use and why you would use them at each stage of the funnel to nurture your leads so that you get the best results from your funnel. Having a successful funnel requires solid execution at each stage of the process.

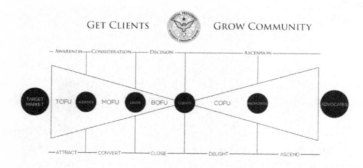

As you review this graphic, notice that there is a difference between the audience and the community. Building an audience is where you start. Your audience can be your email subscribers, blog subscribers, podcast subscribers, YouTube subscribers, social media followers, anybody who is subscribed to get your content on an ongoing basis.

Currently, more than a majority of your audience is not ready to make a purchase.

Therefore, your outcome is to nurture these people in your audience and take them down through your Community Funnel to the point where they buy your product and become fanatics about you and what you do. Once they reach this stage, these people are now part of your community and will eventually become advocates who will do your selling for you by singing your praises to others about what you did to help them.

However, before you can drive people to your funnel and have them come out the bottom as raving fans, you need to determine who you're going to target at the top of the funnel. If you recall, we discussed buyer personas in an earlier chapter. You'll need to identify your buyer personas for each of your products so you can know where to focus on building your audience.

For instance, the four buyer personas for our Inside Sales Product are:

1. Johnny Wanna Hire: Never had an Inside Sales Associate and wants to hire one
2. Will Hadanisa: Has hired an Inside Sales Associate in the past but had no success
3. Al Ready Hasanisa: Has an Inside Sales Associate but wants to get better results than they are currently getting
4. Sam Scale: Has an Inside Sales Person and wants to build a team of Inside Sales Associates

By knowing these personas, we were able to craft a powerful Buyer Journey and attribute the right content to the proper stage of the funnel while addressing each persona's unique needs appropriately to provide value, gain authority, build trust, and subsequently, influence them at the highest level, when appropriate, to do business with us. Essentially, knowing these personas helps us determine how we're going to talk to them.

Let's look at one topic and see how we communicate differently across our four different buyer personas. For this example let's look at "Hiring." Here's what a blog headline might look like for each persona:

Buyer Persona	Content
Johnny Wanna Hire	The 7 Best Times to Hire an ISA for Your Business
Will Hadanisa	How to Hire the Right ISA for Your Team

Al Ready Hasanisa:	5 Strategies to Increase Your ISA's Conversions
Sam Scale:	How To Hire and Manage Multiple ISAs

All of these headlines align with ISA-related information, but they each appeal to a different buyer persona within the overall ISA field.

Putting it All Together

Here are the seven steps you must follow to design and implement a Community Funnel.

1. Create Your Value Journey Canvas

If you recall, your Value Journey Canvas is where you map the journey a client takes and align your Core Content to the stages within the journey. In order to do this properly, as we discussed, you must know your buyer personas and what their Core Desires are.

In order to leverage this strategy, you must first identify your personas' Core Desires. You see, your Core Message will be pervasive throughout the content you deliver in your funnel and it must match your personas' Core Desires. If it doesn't, you don't have a Community Funnel, you have a product funnel, which essentially shoves your prospects, with force, into finding out more about your product (and little to no desire to want to either find out more or buy your product).

Instead, you want your Ideal Client to easily slip into your funnel and continue consuming the content you provide. To accomplish this, you'll want to use a Universal Offer that makes you stand out from your competition, something that differentiates you. You want a call out so that they look at you and your brand and literally say: "That's what I'm looking for; that's exactly what I'm looking for."

When done correctly, prospects are going to end up in the right place. It's like people going out to eat dinner. They aren't going to show up at a place by seeing a sign saying "The Clam Shack" expecting steak when the place only sells seafood. They're going to know that this is or isn't the place for them right out of the gate.

Be very deliberate at this stage of the funnel and make sure that your Core Message and content strategy are in alignment with your buyer personas and their Core Desires. It's the only way that your Community Funnel will succeed in moving prospects into a position where they will buy with you then become a member of your community down the road.

2. Build Your Audience – Top of Funnel (TOFU)

At this phase of the funnel, you're looking to attract the attention of your target market. To accomplish this, you'll use clear messaging to connect with your ideal prospects, segment them, and demonstrate that you can solve their unique problems and provide them with relevant solutions in a way that persuades them to become a subscriber.

When you do this right, you'll create brand awareness and begin a relationship of trust by adding massive value that results in a subscriber.

As you know, we recommend using your book as the Universal Offer to get people into TOFU. A Universal Offer is a low-barrier offer that delivers massive value and appeals to all your buyer personas. When you have an irresistible offer of value, you can easily get your prospects to exchange their information (usually name and email address) for it. In addition to your Universal Offer, you can use content and calls to action from your book to build your audience and get your prospect into TOFU so they can work their way down the funnel.

One way to make your Universal Offer an "irresistible offer" is to give it away for free and just charge shipping and handling. You might be able to charge just enough money to pay for the publication and delivery of your book to your prospect. But if not, it doesn't matter. The goal is to make the offer super juicy so that your prospect can't say no to it. They will pay you with their attention and ultimately with their long-term loyalty as a client.

When we "sell" our book, we give it away for free, and we sell it only for shipping and handling ... a measly $6.95. The goal is to get subscribers and consumption, not to get rich on the book.

The ultimate goal is to generate tens or hundreds of thousands of book buyers without losing money upfront. To accomplish this we implemented a Liquidator Offer. A Liquidator Offer generates a subscriber, lead or a buyer, while simultaneously offsetting the cost of advertising.

Our Liquidator Offers are low-priced, easy-to-consume products that deliver a very specific promise that is complementary to our Universal Offer. Think of them as an add-on or upsell to your Universal Offer. In our Inside Sales Community Funnel, as long as our Liquidator Offer converts at 6 percent, we can give our book away for free and cover all our advertising expenses. This strategy alone helped us sell thousands of books without spending any money to build our audience and acquire new clients.

At TOFU, you're looking to attract a much larger audience of subscribers without trying to discourage people from entering your funnel. The funnel will weed out the insincere and inappropriate prospects.

At the same time, you're going to engage in consistent, relevant communication. Your audience has problems and your job is to communicate to them actual information and solutions that are relevant to what they're looking for. In doing this, you either become a trusted authority or start moving in that direction.

Here are some of the more effective strategies you would use to make compelling offers to prospects in order to get them to want to find out more about you and what you can do to solve their problem(s):

Content Marketing – The vast majority of the buyer's journey is now done digitally. People use the internet to do research regularly before making big decisions. Smart marketers craft and disseminate content like blogs, white papers, e-books, etc., to connect with these people and drive them to their marketing funnel.

To consistently attract your Ideal Client, you must have multiple ways to get their attention. And, while your book is a great Universal Offer, your content will give you the arsenal of angles you need to pull your prospects into your funnel. Angles are all the different ways that you can address your prospects' problems. Each angle should have a compelling headline and a corresponding piece of content that you can use to attract your Ideal Clients. The more angles you have, the more opportunities you have to capture the attention of your prospects.

Great content will create subscribers and keep them coming back for more. You want to select channels that you're comfortable with, but more importantly you want to deliver your content where your prospects are already consuming. Does your Ideal Client read blogs, listen to podcasts, or watch vlogs on YouTube? It's most likely that you'll produce content on multiple platforms, but what's most important is that you start producing content and building your audience now.

Email Marketing – Tracking your results in marketing is paramount if you want to hit the right people with the right message. When you're tracking and identifying what links your prospects are clicking, you can send them the content they want and align the message to their interests. Plus, follow-up emails to build excitement and maintain interest help move them down the funnel to become a buyer.

Webinars – Approximately 66 percent of marketers in the B2B space use webinars and online events as a primary method for generating leads as well as marketing to prospects and customers. Webinars give your prospective clients the opportunity to engage with you for nothing more than a basic registration for the event. Webinars can be prerecorded and played by your prospects at any time, giving them ample opportunity to consume your message and take action.

Search Engine Marketing/Pay-Per-Click – Strategies like search engine optimization (SEO) and pay-per-click (PPC) are extremely effective for enticing visitors to your funnel. If you choose to use these methods to generate leads and subscribers, it's important to track your cost per click (CPC) and your cost per lead (CPL).

Your CPC and your CPL will vary based upon a number of factors, but you'll want to keep it as low as you possibly can. Ultimately, you'll want to use this data in conjunction with the cost of delivering your Liquidator Offer to determine your total customer acquisition cost (CAC). Once you have your CAC, you'll have a much clearer understanding of your profit opportunity on your product or service.

Social Media – Social media is visited frequently by buyers who want information and input on making a purchase. Sharing your content with the users of the various platforms that are out there, you can grab the attention of your prospects and carry on meaningful and engaging conversations with them.

At TOFU, you're simply looking to get a large group of prospects into your funnel. To that end, you'll want what you do to be entertaining, educational, and even inspiring in order to catch people's attention. If you do that well enough, you'll be able to get a large number of people to the next stage of the funnel …

3. MOFU Consumption Campaigns

Your efforts at TOFU have worked and you've created for yourself a throng of excited subscribers who are now considering your product among all the other solutions available to them (including doing it themselves and doing nothing at all).

At this point, you'll start to leverage your Core Content to inform, educate, and entertain your subscribers with content and resources that help them go from where they are to where they want to be, and moves them closer to becoming a client.

This stage of the funnel, MOFU, is the most challenging because there are a lot of people in it that aren't serious buyers. Your goal is to separate the serious from the tire kickers so you can start building credibility with the people who are going to come out of BOFU as serious buyers.

Also, at this point, your prospects still may not realize the extent or scope of their problem, so you really need to help them get clear on what their problem is so you can then illustrate to them how you're going to solve that problem with the perfect solution.

If you do a good enough job at this stage of the funnel, you'll end up with marketing qualified leads (MQL). MQLs are visitors to your website and other parts of your funnel that have demonstrated a significant amount of engagement with you and who are likely to become a paying customer.

An MQL is not to be confused with an SQL (Sales Qualified Lead). An SQL is a lead that's indicated immediate interest in your product and who is ready to make a purchase.

Here are some other main benefits of properly executing your MOFU:

- **More sales with more "now" investment** – Folks will take action and make bigger purchases.
- **Earn the right to be the trusted advisor** – A key to long-term authority
- **Build a deeper relationship** – Leads to a stronger community
- **Speed up the sales cycle** – Make more money sooner.
- **Hone in on interest and pain** – Allows you deliver a better solution, faster, for quicker consumption
- **Drill deeper into your segmentation** – Know your community better to deliver solutions with a better fit.
- **Establish your expertise** – Another huge key to long-term authority
- **Stay top of mind** – Keeps your prospects vested and moving along the funnel
- **Leverage automation** – Work (and sales) get done without you.
- **Build predictable pipelines** – Build sales and revenue you can count on.

Don't forget that you must always deliver expertise, entertainment, and value at all stages of the funnel to keep your prospects engaged and moving closer to making a purchase and becoming a member of your community. Also, remember that at MOFU you usually have only an email address and a first name. You'll need to do some more work so you can capture more information on your prospect.
Here's a peek at some of the stronger strategies for executing MOFU at the highest level.

Email Marketing – This approach allows you to segment the list of those who've made it this far and do some targeted marketing for further segmentation and to encourage opt-ins from the more serious potential buyers. As with TOFU, you can use email to align your messages with the interests, needs, and wants of your prospects.

Call To Action (CTA) – Call to action is a simple digital strategy to capture additional information from your prospects through a web form. By delivering additional content to people in MOFU—webinars, premium content, special offers, free downloads, etc.—you can get them to provide more information about themselves, including their level of interest and what they're looking for from you. CTAs are a simple but effective way to initiate engagement with an interested person.

Landing Pages – Landing pages provide you with a concrete place to take your prospects for the purposes of pitching them on taking a specific action. Your CTAs will usually take your prospects to a landing page. On a landing page, you can provide additional useful content, capture even more leads, get people to sign up for other events like webinars and premium content, and increase your click-through and capture rates with customized pages and forms pre-populated with your prospect's personal information.

Nurturing – With roughly half of your prospects still not ready to make a purchase, you'll need to continue forging and strengthening relationships with people at MOFU. The clearer you are on your ICP and what makes them tick, the easier it is for you to align and deliver messaging that speaks to the people who are "on the fence" but are still Ideal Clients for your product or service. You can use newsletters, offers of ongoing webinars, white papers, educational resources, swipe files, checklists, software downloads, coupons, quizzes, surveys, etc., to keep your ICP engaged and you top of mind with them until they are ready to buy.

A good MOFU is going to capture the information you need to really speak to your prospects' needs and desires to solve their problems. In doing this, the MOFU will also prime your prospects through a solid nurturing strategy to make them an MQL who is on the verge of making a purchase from you.

In order to solidify the decision to be a buyer in the mind of your prospect, you'll need to take them through the processes in the last part of the funnel ...

4. BOFU Conversion Campaigns

At this point in the funnel, it's crucial that you don't short sell the value of your product and service. The solution(s) you offer must be positioned as being superior to those offered by your competitors. In addition, you must speed up the rest of the buying cycle and help your prospect feel confident that they are making the absolute best purchase for their needs.

Success at this stage of the funnel means that you must get your subscribers to suspend their beliefs so they can take action. You must also address their skepticisms by using proof to demonstrate and validate that you can help them achieve their goal. If you can do these things at the bottom of the funnel as they're consuming even more content, you'll have people that binge consume, so they'll go right to the bottom and become buyers.

Here's a look at how your BOFU operates to bring home the sale:

Convert – At this stage, you can either have your salespeople convert the sale or have it done automatically by your technology. Suffice it to say that the higher the ticket price is, the more likely a person will have to come in to close the sale. Having access to the data that's been collected throughout the funnel in a CRM will help your salespeople be effective in not only capturing lightning in a bottle, but also in building rapport on the way to closing the sale.

Ascend – Once you have your client on board, it's time to make sure that their onboarding and user experience is world class. The happiness of your customer is in direct proportion to the level of loyalty you'll experience from them down the road. Your goal is not only to satisfy your client, it's also to get them to stay on board long term and be an advocate for you as part of your community. Raving fans tell their friends, families, and business associates how much they love the products they are using. These positive feelings, when shared en masse, can create new business connections and sales for you (all without your efforts).

To strengthen the loyalty of the members of your community—and to keep them engaged and singing your praises—you'll want to implement a loyalty program that includes things like:

Product & Service Updates – Your product or service may change in function or form. Proactively reaching out to your clients with product and service updates keeps them from experiencing unnecessary problems or gaps in service or production. Doing this will make your clients feel like you are helping them at all turns. They feel valued, which is a good thing if there is a renewal aspect to your product or service.

Special Offers and Upsells – People like to feel like they're getting special treatment from the companies they patronize. Offering existing customers discounts on new products, features, or services will not only make them feel happy and special, it will also help create customers for life. More importantly, these customers will be significant contributors to the long-term growth of your business by the work they do in helping you build your brand through word of mouth.

Content – Buyer's remorse is a real emotion that almost every buyer experiences, especially when making a large purchase. To increase customer satisfaction and to build confidence that they made a solid decision to buy from you, you must continue to send out content that is closely aligned with the product or service they bought. In this stage of the process, you can also use the data you collected about your client through their funnel engagement to create and deliver the most appropriate content.

Your BOFU should provide you with a group of loyalists who are now ready to do your bidding and help you grow your business. Once the sale is made, you need to spend as much time on caring for your clients as you did in preparing to get them to the closing table.

It's easily the most important thing you'll do once you secure your client.

Consider these statistics on retention that Emmet Murphy shared in his book *Leading on the Edge of Chaos*:

- Acquiring new customers can cost as much as five times more than satisfying and retaining current customers.

- A 2 percent increase in customer retention has the same effect as decreasing costs by 10 percent.
- Depending on the industry, reducing your customer defection rate by 5 percent can increase your profitability by 25 to 125 percent.
- (Repeat) business helps the company's bottom line, but it also translates to new opportunities when those satisfied customers advocate on your and your clients' behalf. In short, don't screw up all the hard work you put forth in making the sale by not taking care of your customers once they are in the fold.

5. Offers

Your goal is to have multiple offers that all work together to bring maximum value to your clients and provide maximum profits for you. We've already discussed the Universal Offer (your book) and Liquidator Offers as part of your TOFU strategy to help you build an audience, get subscribers, generate leads, and bring on new buyers profitably. The other offers that round out your Community Funnel are:

- **Core offer** – Your core offer is your core product or service that drives the most revenue for your company.

- **Profit Maximizer** – This is an upsell from your core offer that is highly profitable and designed to increase the Lifetime Value (LTV) of your clients. Profit maximizers can be premium versions of your core product or completely different. When you deliver massive value to your clients, some will want to ascend to a higher level of involvement with you, your product, and your company. Some will want to ascend immediately because they always buy premium products and services. It's important to have a profit maximizer offer even if only a small percentage of your clients can buy. it will have a tremendous impact on your bottom line.

- **Value Net Offers** – Value Net Offers allow you to capture more value from all the other products and services your clients buy. Ask yourself, "What other charges are on my clients' credit card statements?" Can you provide the same products and services to them? Even if you don't want to sell those additional products yourself, you can form affiliate relationships and joint venture partnerships with other companies and make money from every client you refer to them.

When you set up your offers at this stage of the process and in this manner, you can achieve the following results:

- **Universal Offer for every buyer persona** – The more targeted, the more effective they are.
- **Have an unlimited ad budget** – You can use revenue from your faster-selling, lower-cost offers to reinvest in more advertising and lead generation.

- **Acquire customers profitably** – You'll spend less money to acquire customers and reap higher profits on sales.
- **Increase LTV** – Stronger offers of great products attract happier buyers who stay with you longer.
- **Capture more value** – Not only will clients stay with you longer, they'll work hard to find others to become members of your community.
- **Build strong joint venture partners** – Great products that produce solid revenues will want to be sold by joint venture partners and they pay you to sell theirs.

6. Sales Process

Create a seamless, high-conversion sales process that adds value and throughout the process creates happy customers with a desire to not only consume more, but also remain a part of your community.

Sales should be superfluous if you've done marketing right.

People will want to do business with you and there won't be any arm twisting or high-pressure sales tactics. If you put in a lot of heavy lifting and have to put the squeeze on your salespeople to try to generate customers, it's because you have financial goals in lieu of having a good Community Funnel. Conversely, when you have predictability and you have a consistent flow of ready-to-buy clients, it's because you have an audience of people that know, like, and trust you and you have offers that solve real problems.

7. Community

A properly executed Community Funnel will provide you with a growing community of loyal followers that love you, your brand, and everything you do for them. This community will be comprised of like-minded people who rally around a common purpose. It's a place where they like to share and have conversations with other people. With your community, you turn transactional relationships into more emotional relationships that help grow your community even bigger and stronger. It's a mutually-beneficial, reciprocal relationship that will transform your life and business forever.

Environment Is Stronger Than Will

Here's just little more about the importance of building a community.
Once you have a community built around your company, product, and solution, you now have a sales force that will work hard to get you sales without you doing anything more than taking good care of the members of that community.

With a community, your customers are participating in the creation of content. They're sharing success stories and rallying around the one thing you represent.

Your community is going to be something that has its own name, events, and even its own jargon. There's shared narrative in your community and usually a shared value system too. Sometimes there will be shared rituals, even a shared pooling of resources within community.

It takes on a life of its own.

The most important part about your community is that it continues without you. It continues without your content, without your incentives, without the value you as an individual bring to them.

If you were to stop providing content and material to an audience, it would go away.

We're not advocating you stop communicating with your community, but we just want you to know that it's a living, breathing organism that will exist well beyond your initial efforts.

One of the best examples of how a community works is CrossFit. CrossFit has built an amazing, tight-knit community.

Sports Psychologist and CrossFitter Jack Blake describes the community in this way:

The sense of community at CrossFit is unique; everyone knows one another, there is always someone to help with technique, you compare WOD (workout of the day) results, discuss competitions, etc. This doesn't happen in regular gyms, no one speaks to one another except to occasionally ask "are you using this?" At CrossFit you know names, life stories … you know the people, they are your people.

CrossFit doesn't depend on any one instructor or personal trainer. The community works together to support and improve itself. Most importantly, it works to keep people vested and onboard, giving community members a significantly longer lifetime value.

Disjointed marketing efforts get you scattered and inconsistent results. In order to get predictable, consistent and recurring income, you must design a funnel that takes someone from being an ice-cold prospect to becoming an ardent supporter without you needing to talk to this person until the time is right.

Strong funnels are created with purpose and each part of the funnel—TOFU, MOFU, and BOFU—works independently and with the other parts of the funnel to produce high-quality MQLs that are teed up for a sale.

Having your book written gives you not only the content you need to build your funnel properly, but also it's a great Universal Offer to get the people in your funnel started along the journey to becoming your biggest fan.

See **The Process For Getting New Members To Your Community Daily** at
digitalpresident.com/resources

CHAPTER 11

BRAND POWER VS. FORCE

———

"Brand is just a perception, and perception will match reality over time."

—Elon Musk

When most people think of a brand, the first thing that comes to their mind is the company's logo and colors: the Golden Arches, the red and white Target, the big orange Home Depot block letters, etc. Certainly these distinguishing characteristics help with the immediate recognition of the company and the brand itself.

Who among us hasn't been starving on the road and looked longingly into the distance hoping to see those iconic Golden Arches peeking out above the tree line? Right?

But the brand—specifically your brand—has powers that go far beyond the color scheme and font that you choose for its image.

Your brand has the ability to create a very specific perception and send a message that will speak to the people you want to attract and retain as clients.
It also has the capacity to drive how much people will value your business and product(s) and what they'll pay for it now (and keep paying for it long into the future).

More importantly, your brand has the power to elicit feelings and emotions from people, which will also impact the perceived value of your company. When created and positioned properly, your brand can cause people to pay more for your products, even if what you're selling appears to be the same product people can get someplace else.

Here's an example:

MBA students and their professor at the Kellogg School of Management conducted a study to determine the impact of brand on the amount people would be willing to pay for a specific product. The class was broken up into three groups and presented with a specific buying scenario.

The results were eye opening, but very telling at the same time.

Group 1 was asked what they would pay for a good-quality pair of 18-karat gold earrings and the brand of the store was not mentioned. Group 2 was asked the same question, but it was told the earrings were from Tiffany Jewelers. Group 3 was asked the same questions, but it was told the earrings were from Walmart.

The average price for the earrings bought from the unbranded store was $550. The average price increased to $873—an increase of almost 60 percent—when the name Tiffany Jewelers was introduced. The only thing that changed between groups was the name Tiffany. With the Walmart brand added to the mix, Group 3 gave an average price of just $81. That's a nosedive of 85 percent from the unbranded example and an even larger decline of 91 percent from the Tiffany brand.

As you can see, not only does the power of a brand shape a buyer's perception, but also "good quality" means something entirely different between brands depending on their perceived value … even with the same product.

Let's unpack this a little bit.

When you think about Walmart, what is the message that the Walmart brand has in the marketplace: everyday low prices. That's what you see in their commercials because that's the messaging they put out into the market.

Low prices are part of their value proposition; they are the expectation the consumer has when they walk through the front doors of a Walmart.

For the purposes of clarity, a value proposition is a coherent statement that details for consumers how your product solves their problems or makes their situation better while delivering specific benefits to them in using your product. At the same time, it differentiates you and your product from the completion and tells consumers why they should buy from you and not from the competition.

From Walmart's perspective, consumers being able to buy about 142,000 products at the lowest price possible is a huge value proposition and one that helps them haul in just under $500 billion in revenues per year. That's roughly six times what Target brings in annually.

Walmart's ICP buys into the "Everyday Low Prices" message and as such, they're going to apply that filter to everything that they purchase or everything that Walmart has to offer.

When they buy something, they expect it to be low price. This is a great thing for Walmart, but not such a great thing for its competitors (which is another great thing for Walmart, by the way).

Knowing that your brand, its perception, and your messaging have such immense powers, you have to be very clear about what your value proposition is in the marketplace and how that relates to price, service level, and the product that you provide.

For example, if your brand and your positioning is around high quality, exclusivity, and luxury, then your products and services should be priced in a way that would reinforce that. At the same time, your consumer should see brand messaging that illustrates congruency between the messaging of high quality, exclusivity, and luxury, and the pricing structures and service level you offer. This strategy not only applies to the marketing and positioning of your products and services, your company and yourself, but also to the actual delivery of those products and services as well.

Focusing on building your brand is hugely important in growing a successful company. First, it will have a huge impact on increasing the value of your company. As well, it will inspire your employees to work harder and smarter in the direction that serves your brand best. Plus, it also makes acquiring new customers much, much easier.

When constructed properly, your brand strategy should position you as the only viable solution to your customer's problem and be in complete alignment with your ICP's Core Desire.

Building the right brand can be the difference between monstrous success and disastrous failure. As well, it allows your brand to wield immense powers in getting the masses who follow you to take action without you having to force them to do it.

The good news is that we're going to show you how to do it right here.

What Do You Stand For (And Why It Matters)

Before we get too far ahead of ourselves, we'd like to define what a "brand" is.

A brand represents the sum of people's perceptions of a company's customer service, reputation, advertising, and logo. The more clearly the aggregate of these criteria articulates a company's value proposition (what's in it for me and how is this going to make my life better), the easier it will be for consumers to 1) see what it stands for, and 2) align themselves with its mission, purpose, and goals.

In order to make it clear to consumers what your brand represents, you'll want to go through a challenging but rewarding self-discovery process by asking these questions:

- What is your company's mission?
- What are the Features and Benefits (FaBs) of your products or services?
- What do your customers and prospects currently think of your company?
- What are the qualities you want them to correlate with your company?

Make sure you do your research. Also, take the time to understand at a very deep level the needs, habits, and desires of your current and prospective customers. Most importantly, don't assume you know what they think. Make sure you absolutely know what they think.

By doing this, you'll be able to clarify your messaging so that people know what you help them do, how your product is going to make their lives better, and what they need to know in order to purchase your product … and you'll help them make the decision to buy your product faster.

The clearest messenger wins and they position themself in the marketplace so people can understand in a split second how this messenger can help them solve their problems.

If your message is too confusing, your prospects' brains will shut down. People are not programmed to buy the best products and services, they are programmed to buy the ones they can understand the fastest and easiest. Every piece of information you share is like an eight-pound bowling ball to your consumers. The more confusing the information is and the harder it is for your prospect to see how this information is going to solve their problem, the harder it is for them to retain the information and respond positively to the message.

To make things worse, if you use any sort of insider language or completely miss the mark on your message—something which we've all been guilty of—you will make that bowling ball feel like it's slathered in grease and impossible to hold onto, causing you to lose people.

You understand your product at a very high level, but your client doesn't. You need to be able to take the information down to a level where your customers understand your brand/offer/product so they can buy it.

We have to look no further than Dollar Shave Club for an example of this. Their brand message is simple: "Shave time, Shave money." It's straightforward and it tells you everything you need to know about what the company brings to the table: shaving products that save you time and money. Nothing more, nothing less.

It completely represents the overall tone of the brand.

The fact of the matter is that whether or not Dollar Shave Club has the best razors doesn't matter; their message is clear and it resonates with a very large audience.

Also, when you have the clearest message and it's 1) congruent with your ICP's wants, desires, and dreams, and 2) easy for your ICP to understand how it can solve their problems, you give them the ability to engage with you.

By letting them engage with you, you're giving your consumers the "handles to the luggage."

With the handles to the luggage, your message is easy to understand and your consumers won't let it go. They'll come to you for your solution and feel great that they bought it for themselves. Your solution is the absolute best in their mind and they won't want to let your brand out of their sight; they'll always know what you stand for and they'll keep coming back to you for subsequent purchases.

When your clients have the handles to the luggage, they'll expect you to deliver a specific type of product to them, in a very particular way, at a price that is commensurate with the value you have created for them.

Like your brand and messaging, these expectations are clear. And when they are met, they will inspire a strong sense of allegiance from your clients, causing them to become clients for life who will be willing to pay more for your product than they would elsewhere from someone else.

TOMS Shoes in Playa Del Rey, California gives us a perfect example of this.

In 2006, Blake Mycoskie founded TOMS Shoes. From the outside, TOMS seemed like any other company that had a unique style to them. No frills, just casual shoes that were comfortable to wear.

The thing that stood out, though, is they were sold in higher-end stores like Nordstrom and Saks Fifth Avenue and they were probably priced a little bit above what the perceived value could have been for those shoes.

Upon closer inspection, you discover that the brand—TOMS Shoes—was anchored in the purpose of donating a pair of shoes to a poor child for every new pair of shoes that were sold. That strategy, "One for One," is part of their mission and it is a huge part of what their brand represents: social equity.

Consumers who love TOMS know what they stand for, so they have an expectation when they're buying TOMS that they are going to be paying a little more for their shoes, and they do it with pleasure.

The same will happen with you, your products, and your company. As consumers come to expect things from your strong brand, it moves your product from relative elasticity to relative inelasticity when it comes to price. More specifically, demand is unaffected by price increases.

And TOMS Shoes proves this point: people might look at a pair of TOMS Shoes and have an expectation for a lower price, however because of what TOMS represents and what they stand for, people are willing to pay more for that particular product.

When you position your company and product properly and control your message and consumers' perception of them in the marketplace, you can collect top dollar because people will pay for it. And, when you link your positioning to what you are and what you stand for (something that is tied specifically to the Core Beliefs that your ICP shares with you and your company), your brand will be strong and absolutely invaluable.

Another way to say this is you have brand equity. Brand equity can be distilled into three categories:

1. Customer Perception – How do customers see your product and do they feel like it's the best solution for their specific situation? Do they see your company in a positive light and would they recommend you to others? Are you viewed as the only solution for the majority of consumers?

2. The Effect the Perception Has on Your Company – If there is a positive perception, do consumers come back to purchase again? Do they tell others about your company and recommend to people that they buy from you? Conversely, if the perception is negative, do they not purchase or only purchase once and never again? Do they persuade others not to do business with you?

3. The Value of this Effect – Are people willing to pay more for your product than they would for the same product at another company? Do they continue to purchase from you, even if prices go up? Will they do legwork for you in an effort to help you get sales (even without you asking for their assistance)?

The stronger your brand is and the better it performs in the eyes of the consumer, the more valuable it is. And although this goes without saying, we're going to say it anyway: The more valuable your brand is, the more people are going to pay for your product.

It's why people will pay 91 percent more for 18-karat gold earrings at Tiffany's.

If your brand equity is not as valuable as you would like, you take the following actions to improve on it:

Understand your ICP at the highest level – You must target your ICP properly and deliver tremendous value in their eyes. They are not looking for you to be the hero. They want to be the hero. They want you to be the "guy" or the "gal" who can help them get what they want while still letting them be the hero.

Develop and strengthen your company's marketing and advertising strategies – What you say, how you say it, and where you say it all need to be delivered professionally with a significant amount of impact on your ICP's mind and emotions. If you cannot sway your ICP to take action, you cannot improve your brand equity.

Crush your Customer Journey at all turns of the funnel: TOFU, MOFU and BOFU – You are looking to build raving loyalists out of the people who love you. Not only will they buy from you, but they'll help get others to do the same thing. The Value Journey and Value Exchange must not fail in getting people out of BOFU and into your community if you want a valuable brand equity.

To understand the value of your brand and what it brings to the bottom line, you only need to look to one of the most iconic brands on the planet, Coca-Cola.

Coke's Market Capitalization (Market Cap) without brand value is $50 billion. When you add in the brand value, the Market Cap almost triples to $120 billion. The brand, alone, is worth more than all of its physical assets. Coke has built a hugely powerful brand equity and as a result, it can charge more for its products and capture a huge share of the market.

The more you do to strengthen your brand through the clarity of the message you deliver to your ICP, the more you will drive up the value of the brand itself.

Your Brand Strategy Hard at Work

With a powerful brand, you don't need to force consumers to do business with you. Hence the title of the chapter, Brand Power vs. Force. When created strategically, your brand should easily and effectively influence the right people to choose to do business with you. More importantly, it should position you as the only viable solution for your ICP.

Your brand strategy can be defined as the how, what, where, when, and to whom you plan on sharing and following through on delivering on your brand promise. Your strategy is not limited to your product, though. Where you market and advertise falls under brand strategy. The different places people can consume your product and/or services constitute brand strategy. The images and words you use are all part of your brand strategy.

As part of building out your strategy, you'll want to define your brand promise. In defining your brand promise, you'll want to start with this simple question: "What do you do and for whom do you do it?" You have to think about the promise you're making and how it's going to make someone's life better, richer, happier, healthier, easier, etc.

Once you have that squared away, consider these other steps to define your brand promise:

1. Keep it simple – It should able to be understood from a one- or two-sentence statement that captures your company's mission in the form of a tagline: "The Ultimate Driving Machine," "Think Different," and "We are Harley Davidson" are some of the better-known brand promises.

2. Make sure it's credible – Your consumer's experience must correspond with your brand promise, or the value of your brand is diminished. Ford realized this the hard way when it had to change its brand promise from the 1980s. It used to be "Quality is Job 1," but with so many repairs required and the "Ford – Fix Or Repair Daily" brand promise consumers created, they changed the brand promise to "Go Further."

3. Be Different – This falls under your value proposition. Your brand promise should distinguish you from your competition. GEICO's "15 minutes or less can save you 15 percent or more on car insurance" set the insurer apart from the pack and catapulted them to the top of the auto insurance industry.

4. Make it Memorable – Your brand promise should influence every aspect of your organization: employees, decisions, interactions with customers—everything. It has to carry enough clout to virtually move mountains for your organization.

5. Make it Inspiring – You want everyone who comes in contact with your brand promise to have some sort of emotional attachment to it. You want that strong, emotional connection in order to inspire people. Nike even tells you it wants to inspire you: "To bring inspiration and innovation to every athlete in the world."

The stronger your brand promise is, the stronger your brand will be and the more it will resonate with your ICP, leading them to see your company as the one and only solution to their problem.

What's also part of your brand strategy is the congruence between all of the elements of your strategy, your promise, and your communication with your consumer. The messaging should be clear, consistent, and evident in all aspects of your overall brand image.

You want congruency not just for the purposes of clarity, but also to maintain transparency with your ICP. Your followers are going to see you in webinars, on Instagram, Twitter, Facebook, hear you on podcasts, and read a ton of content that you produce.

Your branding strategy demands congruency—congruency in messaging, in your personal brand, in the words that you and your brand own, in the visuals you use, and in the promise you make on which your ICP is going to take you up. You also must be congruent with your ICP, their beliefs about themselves and about what they think you can do to help them.

Your congruency must be authentic at all times because being perceived as inauthentic, fake, and even as a poser will crush your brand.

Most importantly, your congruency will provide for the connection and engagement you want and need from consumers.

For instance, take George Foreman and his endless line of indoor and outdoor grills. Foreman was an Olympic gold medalist and a WBA heavyweight champion boxer. He was never the leanest or most muscular boxer, but he did have cachet as a champion and one of the toughest guys on the planet.

Also, what most people don't know is that Foreman ate two hamburgers before every boxing match and had four sons whose favorite food—you guessed it—is hamburgers.

At the time, the parent company, Salton, had a brand promise for the grill: "Lean, Mean, Fat-Reducing Grilling Machine" and Foreman was a spot-on match for the brand. In addition, as a successful athlete and father himself, his personal brand was completely congruent with the ICP for the grill: someone who thought of themselves as a successful person who enjoyed grilled food, wanted to be on the healthy side, but wasn't looking to be a bodybuilder or a complete health nut in doing so.

The results of this brand strategy speak for themselves: Salton began selling the grills with Foreman's help in 1995, and by 1998 it had sold over $200 million worth. The grills had been selling so well that a year later the company felt it could be even more profitable if it bought Foreman out, so they stroked him a check for $137.5 million (worth almost $200 million in today's dollars). In the end, over 100 million grills were sold.

Had Foreman not resonated so deeply with the grill's consumers and had the brand, the brand promise, and Foreman not been congruent with each other and the wants, dreams, and desires of the ICP the grill targeted, the Salton company would have never succeeded like it did.

You Must Get Emotionally Involved

In order to continue increasing the value of your brand, your strategy must create some form of emotional attachment for your consumer. For example, Nike connects its product lines with star athletes in the hope that consumers will transfer their emotional attachment from their favorite athlete to the actual product sold by Nike.

Selling the shoe goes way beyond just the shoe at Nike; they want to connect to their consumers at an emotional level.

To connect successfully with your ICP—and motivate them to use, connect, and stay with your brand—you must speak to one of their six core human needs. These are not simply wants and desires, they are deep-seated needs that represent the foundation of every choice we make.

The six core needs are: certainty, variety, significance, love and connection, growth, and contribution. The first four needs are considered to be "needs of the personality" and the last two needs are known as "needs of the spirit."

In 1943, psychologist Abraham Maslow identified these needs in a paper entitled "Theory of Human Motivation" that he wrote for *Psychological Review*. Personal development expert Anthony Robbins has taken those needs and identified what motivating factors play into each of the six needs.

Let's break them down a little here:

1.   Needs of the personality (needs of personality and achievement)

a.   Certainty – People looking for certainty want control, stability, consistency, comfort, and predictability.

b.   Uncertainty or Variety – Those who want uncertainty or variety like challenges, surprises, excitement, adventure, and even a little chaos. Certainty and Uncertainty work to even each other out. A significant lack of one will often require rebalancing by the other.

c.   Significance – This is the need to feel important, valued, meaningful, wanted, and worthy of love.

d.   Love and Connection – Here, people are looking for unification with another, communication, approval, attachment, and literally, connection with another person.

Significance and Love and Connection are also at odds with each other. The more someone focuses on meeting their own needs, the harder it is to meet the needs of a spouse or mate.

2.   Needs of the spirit (needs for fulfillment and happiness)

a.   Growth – Here, people are desirous of emotional, intellectual, and spiritual improvement and development.

b.   Contribution – This is the need to give to others, serve mankind, and protect those other than ourselves.

We all have these needs, and the first four can be met in both constructive and destructive manners. Your goal in creating your brand strategy is to have your brand speak to the needs of those you are trying to influence.

You can't just wing it. You must be deliberate in designing your brand strategy and you absolutely have to get your ICP emotionally involved with your brand.

A good example of this would be Shaquille O'Neal and Icy Hot.

The people who use Icy Hot are looking for some certainty in their lives. By using Icy Hot, they know that their back and muscle pain will go away. As a result of that, they have an emotional attachment to using the product.

By adding Shaquille to the mix, Icy Hot is layering congruency into its brand strategy. Shaq is an older, former professional athlete who likely experienced back and muscle pain while he was playing (and still experiences some today). Many people in their 30s and older have some sort of pain, especially after working out, and want relief from the pain.

Icy Hot's ICP identifies with Shaq's current situation and buys into his solution for his problem at a very high level. So much so that Icy Hot outsells the next brand, Salonpas, by almost 2 to 1 and stomps the original muscle pain reliever, Bengay, 3 to 1.

Your brand strategy is going to take some time to create, but the time invested will be well worth it as you'll be ensuring that your brand and brand promise get the absolute best results for your company. More importantly, it will drive up the value of your brand considerably so that people will not only pay more for your product, but also they'll see you as the absolute best and only choice for their emotional, psychological, and physical needs.

Your Brand Strategy and Your ICP

As we touched on earlier, your brand strategy stems from you. Your Core Philosophy and Core Values are the foundation for the brand promise you make to your consumers. To that end, you have a brand and it will be seen by all who consume your content at every phase of the Customer Journey.

Your personal brand is very powerful and you can harness that power to create tremendous value as long as your brand strategy aligns everything about you and what you do with your ICP, and what they need from you.

Now, you might be asking yourself: "How can my personal brand have such a huge impact on my ICP and my company brand at the same time?" Well, you have to look no further than the Kardashians to find out.

According to *Maxim* online, *US Weekly* and *FHM* magazine recently posted some estimates from Michael Heller, owner of digital marketing company, Talent Resources, for how much Kim, Khloé, and Kourtney haul in for a selfie that properly positions a brand's label: "Brands pay up to $500,000 for a campaign to 36-year-old Kim's 94.8 million Instagram followers, Heller says, while sisters Khloé, 32, and Kourtney, 37, can rack up $250,000 for sharing branded snaps with their 64.1 million and 54.3 million followers, respectively."

Kendall and Kylie Jenner have accounts that are approaching 100 million followers and they could garner as much as $500,000 per individual post.

The Kardashians have so much congruency and clout with their followers that corporate brands pay them astronomical amounts of money simply for posting a picture of themselves wearing those brands.

The crazy thing is that these brands—Chanel, Louis Vuitton, Jimmy Choo, DKNY, etc.—already have brands that are valuable to begin with, yet they tie some of their success to the personal brands of the Kardashians.

Makes you kind of wonder why Kim stays with Kanye, doesn't it?

All kidding aside, no matter how far your company has grown from your personal brand influencing sales and business growth, you need to realize that it's your personal brand consumers are going to be seeing on the different platforms where you distribute content. To that end, you must own and strengthen that personal brand and relate it to your corporate brand to own the strongest amount of mindshare with your ICP.

Now, we've had first-hand experience as an ICP who was influenced by the power of the personal brand and the overall corporate brand.

Several years back there was a consultant who put out a tweet on Twitter that he had never tweeted before. In it, he said he was going to be working with some project clients and the cost was going to be about six figures. He was only going to be working with a couple of clients and that was it.

The sticker shock of six figures was high, but we engaged him to see what the details of the opportunity were mainly because this person's brand was affiliated with something we were looking for. In short, this guy was a legit player in the market and his brand was strong in the space where his expertise lived.

At the time, we had a very specific problem, which was really getting products to market in the online community. There were a lot of players in this space with varying degrees of expertise at the time, but this guy had a reputation of being very good— extremely good—at acquiring customers through a specific methodology for which he had branded himself. That brand promise was how to acquire a large number of clients in a short amount of time.

It was also tied to helping people get that clarity and messaging in marketing in order to be able to do the things that we understand at a very high level now that we really had very little understanding of back then. We understood marketing basics, but we really lacked the knowledge and importance of how all the pieces fit together to engineer a massive online client attraction strategy that got great results.

As a potential ICP, he was speaking our language and we were excited to engage him in further conversation.

Excited to speak with him, we got on the phone with the individual and talked about his services. Michael remembers being on the phone with his business partner who was on the other side of the table and they were looking at each other. As they were talking to him he said, "Listen, I just need to know what you want to do because these are the dates that we'd be getting together and if these dates work, you could just fly with us."

As fate would have it, he was going to be in the same place as we were; he said, "If you decide to do it, you can just fly back with us on the jet, but I need to know because there's only two seats. If y'all are going to come …." Originally, he was going to invite some of his other buddies to tag along with him, but he wasn't going to invite those guys if he was going to let us tag along with him.

Here's where the emotional part of his brand strategy kicked in for us. At that particular time, neither Michael nor his partner had ever flown on a private jet. A switch flipped in their heads as their thought process transitioned from "Are we going to do this?" to "We are going to do this, but we just need to find a way to make it happen."

They wanted what he had: a super-successful real, online marketing business that created generational wealth for his family. His personal brand and his corporate brand were in complete congruence with each other and they both resonated with us at a very high level. His messaging was in complete alignment with our desires and he knew how to solve our problem at a very high level.

He embodied everything that we wanted to be and to have.

Plus, his value proposition was a dead-on match for us and where we wanted to be. It was the perfect storm of opportunity for us and we were prepared to write a six-figure check to take him up on his offer. This piece of information is key because we started off thinking we'd be willing to invest five figures in his services when we first heard of the opportunity.

When your personal brand and corporate brand are in complete congruence with each other and when your brand strategy aligns with your ICP's desires, your brand is so strong and valuable that you can command serious money for what you do. You can even get your ICP to invest more money than they might be originally willing to commit in solving their problem.

The Power of Shared Experiences

It's one thing for your ICP to read about and identify with you and your personal brand. It's an altogether different thing for you and your ICP to share experiences with each other.

Michael and his partner did end up working with that consultant in a different capacity for their online marketing strategy and they did get to fly in a private jet with him. It was an amazing experience. And, because it was their first time doing so, it was a super-special opportunity that connected them to him at a very deep level. The connection became so strong that they ended up investing thousands of dollars over the next ten years to learn from and work with him on other projects.

The power of shared experiences is real. Whether you do podcasts and webinars where your ICP can interact with you online, or if you do live, in-person events, you can use shared experiences to strengthen your alignment with your ICP's desires and deepen your personal connection with them.

The key thing to remember here is that sharing experiences doesn't have to be connected to the delivery of your product and service. Remember, your personal brand is a key driver here, so building relationships with your ICP is hugely important and impactful in forging them.

When you're sure to give your ICP access to you and what you stand for as part of your overall brand strategy, amazing things will happen for you and your business.

In the end, you must carefully craft the brand you choose to put out there for the world to see, because it's what your consumers are going to use as a determinant for doing business with you. Your personal brand—which is driven by your Core Purpose and Core Values—will have a huge impact on what your corporate brand shakes out to be in the end.

Knowing what your ICP wants and what you do for them is also a key component of building a successful, sustainable brand. Clarity on that is crucial.

Building the brand is only part of the equation. You must also have a brand strategy that encompasses every aspect of your product from creation to delivery and everything in between … and it all needs to be built around a brand promise that has staying power.

You'll know when you've nailed your personal and corporate brand when it all resonates at a deep level with your ICP and their Core Desires. When it does, your brand will have tremendous value that your ICP will be willing to pay top dollar for.

Download **The Guide To Determine Your Brand Promise** at
digitalpresident.com/resources

DIGITALPRESIDENT.COM/COMMUNITY

CHAPTER 12

COMMUNITY IS THE NEW CURRENCY

"Let another praise you, and not your own mouth; A stranger, and not your own lips.

—PROVERBS 27:2

Anyone can create a product and sell it to people. For that matter, anyone can create a great product and have consumers give it great reviews. But if you're looking to build a business that will stand the test of time and grow beyond your personal efforts, you'll need to build a community of excited, die-hard fans who love you and what you do.

A community is bigger than you are and it's bigger than any one person. It's not created overnight. It takes effort and you must create it strategically for it to have staying power. A properly built community is comprised of members who share the same values and an affinity for a brand's Core Identity (what the brand represents). Through a shared purpose, the members of the community work together to build your brand, recruit new members and generate new and exciting content so that your shared purpose will grow to reach more people than you could ever reach on your own.

Again, there's a lot of hard work that goes into creating a thriving throng of faithful followers, but it's absolutely worth the effort because with a solid tribe, you'll have a strong group of people who will bring new members into the community, sell you and your product or solution on your behalf, and even create content and disseminate it to people who don't even know you exist.

Next to writing your book, it's one of the most important steps in the process of creating an automated, online money-making machine so you can live your Life by Strategy.

Here's what it means to have a powerful community in your corner:

- Massive encouragement when you're thinking of throwing in the towel
- Lots more stamina and initiative than you could ever generate on your own
- Personal growth and development through long-standing relationships
- A frenzied community that will create a path for you to turn your passion into a livelihood
- Most importantly, leading a community gives you the opportunity to make your life, and the lives of those you touch, significantly better.

The best news about forming a community is that the predisposition to form groups, and then to be partial to in-group members, appears to be instinct based. Some feel it's not intuitive: they maintain that favoring in-group members may be more conditioned and not involuntary, like when we as children associate with family and kids from the neighborhood because that's what we learn from our environment to do.

That said, because these relationships with friends, family and neighbors happen with such ease, it can more likely be identified as what psychologists call "prepared learning," the ingrained bias to learn something quickly and unconditionally. Cognitive psychologists have discovered that newborns are partial to their mother's face and to the sounds of their native tongue. As they grow older, they are partial to people who speak their native language within hearing distance. In addition, preschool children are more inclined to pair up with friends who speak their native language.

Social psychologists have gathered results from experiments that show how quickly and decisively we separate into groups and then show favoritism to the one to which they belong. Surprisingly, even when the groups were determined arbitrarily, preference for the group in which the person was placed was extremely prominent. It didn't matter if the group was playing cards or discussing the merits of one book author over another, the members of the group always favored the in-group and its members over the out-group. They viewed the out-group as their opponent or enemy and deemed its members to be not as likeable, not as fair, not as trustworthy, and not as skilled as they were.

The rate and consistency with which the in-group bias occurred was fascinating.

To leverage this practically inborn tribe-builder trait, it's going to be your job to provide the vision, Core Philosophy, and Core Identity for your community and then stoke the fires of excitement within your faithful followers to get that community not only up and running, but also living and breathing on its own (with fervor) … long after you lay the groundwork.

At the same time, if your product or service is going to have any value in the eyes of your customers, it must also meet a functional need. Benefits like saving time and money or providing lots of solid information fill a functional need. There are other needs that can be met, including emotional, life-changing, and social impact that can strengthen your community.

As you work your way up the ladder of human needs and start layering in other factors like wellness, nostalgia, mental and physical wellness, therapeutic value, and provide an atmosphere of affiliation and belonging, your customers will get more value and your community will grow stronger. Plus, as you bring more value to the table, you can charge more for your products and services. It's a classic win-win scenario.

Here's an example of what a highly effective, extremely passionate, dyed-in-the-wool community looks like.

In 1984, the Boston Celtics and the Los Angeles Lakers met for the National Basketball Association (NBA) World Championship. That series, which went seven games, has been called the single best championship series in NBA history, as the event had more twists and turns than a roller coaster at Six Flags Over Texas.

The Celtics finally bested the Lakers on a June night that year and the battle cry for the faithful dressed in green was "Celts Supreme!" Social psychologist Roger Brown was there to observe the aftermath:

The fans burst out of the Garden and nearby bars, practically break dancing in the air, stogies lit, arms uplifted, voices screaming. The hood of a car was flattened, about thirty people jubilantly piled aboard, and the driver—a fan—smiled happily … It did not seem to me that those fans were just sympathizing or empathizing with their team. They personally were flying high. On that night, each fan's self-esteem felt supreme; a social identity did a lot for many personal identities.

The Celtics fans were a community that got behind a shared purpose: winning the NBA World Championships and redeeming themselves from the embarrassment of getting swept in the prior year's championship series.

More than that, they were a community that bought into the Celtics' Core Identity (read: what a brand represents)—winning championships. The win in 1984 was their 15th and it represented one-third of all the NBA championships that had ever been won.

You might think that they were just banding together because everyone wants to be associated with a winner. While you might be right, that's only a small part of the reason those fans were so rabid. We'll explain more a little later on in the chapter.

First, let's take a look at a more recent example.

UFC fighter, Conor McGregor, and boxing legend, Floyd Mayweather, had an epic fight in August of 2017. Floyd Mayweather had already proven himself to be a world-beater to the boxing audience by going 49–0, which explains why he was a heavy favorite to win the fight.

That notwithstanding, the UFC community was bigger and stronger than that of the boxing world. Its passionate support of McGregor was the real story here.

Prior to this fight, the biggest pay-per-view event ever happened on May 2, 2015 when Floyd Mayweather fought—and beat—Manny Pacquiao. The event drew 4.4 million viewers on pay-per-view and hauled in $400 million in revenue.

By himself, McGregor was already the biggest pay-per-view draw in UFC history. He holds records at 1.65 million (UFC 202), 1.5 million (UFC 196), and 1.3 million (UFC 205). For the fight between him and Mayweather, the total viewers came in at just over 4.4 million and the total revenue was approximately $620 million (nearly $200 million more than the brand value for the NFL Super Bowl).

The power wielded by the UFC community extended way beyond that. It could also be seen in how the odds in Las Vegas changed dramatically from the time the odds were first set to what they were at the time of the fight. Twice as much money was bet on this fight compared to what was laid out for the Mayweather vs. Pacquiao tilt. As well, there were six bets of $1 million, which was five more than were made on the New England Patriots vs. Atlanta Falcons in February of 2017.

Not to mention, McGregor started as a 7–1 underdog for the fight, but as the UFC community rallied around him and shared his values of being a brash, hard-nosed fighter who has overcome so many obstacles in his life, the odds dropped to as low as 3.5–1 at one point. This due to the fact that 90 percent of the bets placed were for McGregor to win the fight.

Like the Celtics, McGregor has championships under his belt. However, he doesn't have the championship pedigree that the Celtics have with 17 world championships to their name. Additionally, Floyd Mayweather had a comparably larger amount of success in fighting than McGregor had at the time they fought. Mayweather is someone who had won 15 world titles in five different boxing divisions, and again, was the Vegas favorite with a flawless record.

In the end, Mayweather beat McGregor, but the entertainment value was what people wanted and it's what they got.

What made the Celtics community rally around them was entirely different than what made McGregor's faithful fans fanatical about supporting him. And it will be different when your community supports you and your brand with its hearts and wallets because of you and what you stand for.

It's not just about being a winner, it's about being a winner in the eyes of your tribe—something every business owner wants.

Here's the why, what, and how you need to know in building your own throng of raving fans.

Why You Need to Build a Community

If you think back to Chapter 5, you'll remember we talked about Cialdini's Six Principles of Influence and how social proof and endorsements were a powerful law in influencing people to take action. Word of mouth is—and will always be—the most trusted form of advertising.

In order to grow and lead a thriving community, you must have a strong, clear vision for yourself and others to rally around. Remember, people are coming to you so you can help solve their problems. As well, these people are your ICP, so they already identify with you at some level and they're looking to you for your leadership.

You want them to be passionate about what you're passionate about and buy into your vision at a very deep level. When you can get your community to do that, they will be around for the long haul. If you don't do that, they'll find someplace else to do it or they'll just do it themselves.

Remember, the need to gather together and be part of a tribe is innate—it's virtually part of DNA. Failing to have a strong vision and passion and failing to communicate properly means your community does not grow, and that could signal the death of your automated business.

Our vision for our community members is that they can design and live a Life by Strategy by becoming the Digital President of their niche. By writing a book where they share their Core Philosophy and beliefs—and then strategically creating and implementing a Community Funnel—the members of our community can have an automated business that works around the clock to help them grow sales and create their own communities.

We want people to live the life of their dreams and build a community that helps them add value and change the lives of people that they could never impact on their own. This part bears repeating: You must create a super-compelling vision that's tied in with your passion. Your job is to create a compelling vision as it relates to your passion. Please note that while supplying the vision is on you, it really has almost nothing to do with you. Your vision must be bigger than you and it must be inspiring. When—and only when—you do this, will you be able to spawn and grow a powerful community.

As your community continues to grow and take on a life of its own, the members will start having experiences that will create emotional connections with you, your product or service, and each other. These experiences will be rich in authenticity, helping members form bonds that will make the community brim with excitement, excitement that people will want to keep experiencing ... excitement that people will want to share with others that they know, like, and trust who can be potential members for your community.

What's even better is that the members of your community will also be more comfortable with each other and, more importantly, you. This is a good thing because it allows them to engage in an open and real manner with you and each other.

Open and real means that you not only get feedback, but also that you get feedback that is meaningful and usable by you. Open communication and a solid feedback loop allows you to provide better service, make changes to your product and service that will be useful to consumers, deliver more impactful and helpful content, create new products and/or services that meet a specific need, improve retention within the community, and most importantly, to continue to build trust with your community.

One of the ways to create an open and real environment is to give your members a chance to talk. To make the process of engagement simple, provide them with an online form or hold a live social event. If you can, wait 24 hours before you give your two cents on questions that are asked within the group, even if you have the answer. This is important because it's more important that your community members connect with—and have discussions with—each other to build relationships and trust. Sometimes, conversations will come to a screeching halt when you go in and answer questions right off the bat because people may not feel comfortable weighing in since you're viewed as a strong authority.

You want to try to get your members interacting with each other and forming those emotional relationships if you want your community—and business—to succeed.

It's important you know your community is not a standard marketing audience. If you're posting blog posts, videos, podcasts, and other content and you're not creating or encouraging discussions, you have a traditional marketing audience—you produce, they consume, and it's mostly you talking to them. The community magic happens when the conversation is predominantly between the members of your group (with or without your interactions).

Here are a few tips to help you maintain an environment of engagement where feedback is both encouraged and accepted:

- Talk to your community like you are a regular person – It's okay if everything is not grammatically correct.
- Be available to your community – Make sure you answer emails and respond to posts in a reasonable period of time.

- Be vulnerable to your community – It's okay to show them that you're not perfect.

We're not saying they need to know your deepest, darkest secrets (or what you eat for breakfast, lunch, and dinner). You just want to be the most authentic version of you.

When you do that, the magic will happen.

What's incredible is that as you master this aspect of building a community, you can optimize the results you're getting through an "excite and ascend" strategy. Once the sale is made, you give your members the opportunity to get excited about your product and aiding them in learning to use it better so they can ascend. If they have a positive experience, they're likely going to want to make subsequent purchases from you. In fact, building your community and approaching growing it in this manner could grow your return on investment by a factor of 10 times when done properly.

An example of this is strategy can be seen in the company Watch Gang. Watch Gang is an online subscription service where subscribers get a watch each month and use the company's Facebook group. Watch Gang does this to provide their customers with an environment where they can have a great experience with their products. If consumers are not satisfied with a particular watch, they can join this group, engage with other customers, and work out trades.

A strong, thriving tribe will take your business (and your life) in directions that you never thought were possible. Through a strong ethic of adding value, being authentic and human in your communication, keeping people engaged and creating powerful emotional connections, you and your community will touch so many lives in such a positive way, even without you having to be the one who makes the most impact.

What Does a Solid Community Look Like?

For the purposes of being Digital President, your community is a gathering of like-minded individuals that has an outlet on the internet. As with a physical community, your community members will get together to share common interests.

Any successful community has attributes that denote membership or affiliation with it. It will be the same for your community.
Earlier in this chapter we talked about the Celtics and Conor McGregor and how their tribes are rabid, my-team-right-or-wrong communities who identify with them at a variety of levels.

If we take an even deeper look, we see that their respective communities identify so strongly with them that when the team wins, they take credit along with the team and even take credit for the triumph themselves.

Conversely, when their team loses, they, too, feel the pain and loss associated with the defeat. A win for their team is a win for them and a loss for their team is a loss for them.

It's a very powerful connection they share, and their affinity for you and your company is all part of the culture within your community.

Your tribe is just like a team: a unified group of players (women and men) who are linked by the vision and passion you've shared with them. Just as with communities of sports teams, your community lives and dies with you based on the successes and failures it experiences.

To build a killer community and leverage the connection your members have with you and each other, you'll want to craft your own language and a Core Identity that your tribe members can latch onto and make part of who they are.

Our members understand the impact and importance of being the Digital President in their niche. They know that their book and Community Funnel are what separate them from their competition. They share in the pride of being able to live a Life by Strategy because they're the Digital President—the absolute expert—in what they do. For them, it's more than just being self-employed or an entrepreneur, it's about owning the space in which they exist and providing the best solution out of anyone who does the same thing they do.

We also have language like "carnival marketer." If you remember, a carnival marketer is someone who has no strategy or value to offer and is just looking to make a sale. We also have "Ideal Client Profile," "Community Funnel," "Life by Strategy," and "Core Philosophy" as language that's specific to our community.

In our real estate community, we use the term "Average Frustrated Agent" or "AFA" to talk about real estate agents in the marketplace who are working their butts off, only to sell a small number of homes while adding little to no value to the lives of their prospects and clients.

The phrase was pervasive in our community and we would often get calls from coaching prospects who would tell us point blank: "We don't want to be AFAs anymore. How can you help us?" It was powerful language and the folks who worked with us or wanted to join us made it part of their vernacular.

Phrases and words like these work in conjunction with our Core Identity to form a glossary of terms used within our community. You can and should do the same for yours.

The other language we have that's specific to our tribe is how we identify members and those looking to become members. Yes, all communities start with someone in a leadership position, but they grow and thrive because of the people who are part of them.

There are three types of people we have within our community and all of them are vital to the success and growth of the community itself:

Advocates: These folks are die-hard supporters of your cause and the warriors of your community. Without you asking them, your advocates will support your platform and share everything they can about you, your business, and what you do. They buy virtually everything you sell and share every piece of content and free stuff you give them so that they can expose people to you. They will do whatever it takes to make you and the community successful. They stand out from the crowd and are people you can count on to help keep your community strong.

Advocates like to be recognized and rewarded for their efforts. Offering fringe benefits like access to early releases of your products, being test cases for your newest creations, and pointing out how incredible they are to the overall community go a long way in keeping your advocates happy and engaged. Their success is your success and they love for you to share that on the social media platforms that you use to communicate with your tribe.

Promoters: These people love you and what you do. They will sing your praises to everyone and anyone who will listen. They've had great success dealing with you and in using your product or service. In addition to that, they have high levels of influence and are often leaders in the larger market within your niche. In some cases, they may have more influence with consumers in your space, but that's a good thing as you're looking to them to spread the good word about you. Because they buy into your shared value and purpose, they will be great supporters and key members of your community. As well, you can leverage them to bring new people by using their platforms to talk about you and what you do.

Your goal is to add as much value to them in their businesses and help in ways that they may not be as strong as you are. Reciprocity is a key element in working with your advocates. The more success you help them achieve by filling in the gaps for where they are weak, the more they will work to help you build your community.

Prospects: Prospects are the lifeblood of any growing community and you need a consistent flow of them to expand your tribe.

Your book and funnel will do the best job of getting prospects through your Customer and Value Journey on their way to becoming members of your community. That said, the hard work of your Advocates and Promoters will also be a key element of bringing Prospects to the table.

Your community, when built correctly, will be the heart and soul of your business.

How Do You Build a Successful Community?

Your shared purpose, shared values, and Core Identity are the foundation of a thriving community. The stronger those three things are and the better job you do of forming and communicating them, the more successful and magnetic your tribe will be.

Once you get your community up and running, you will need a solid strategy to build a culture that fosters connection with you and its members. That strategy exists in the quantity and quality of engagement in which you and your tribe participate. Your success also rests in the quality of people you bring into your community and how hard you work in the beginning to get people excited and vested in making the community great.

Here are a few things to consider when building your community:

1. Communities are not rockets … they are not launched

Much like a plant, communities start with a seed that is planted. They grow organically and ultimately turn into a movement.

At some point, you may make an announcement that the community exists, but it's not what you would do at the very beginning. You must set your foundation, as we mentioned above, which will set the tone for the people who get involved with your tribe. The right people—your ICP—will identify with your philosophy and messaging and rally around it. Soon, the frenzy will spill over and they'll be inviting others to join them (and you) to help the community grow from a smoldering pit of coal to a huge, roaring flame of excitement about what's going on in your community.

Starting small with a great foundation allows you to control the culture and quality of interaction that develops in the community.

2. Your community is not for everyone

If you want your community to be a place where people are going to keep coming back to, you want to make sure that the quality of each person in the community is high. We all have a certain amount of time, and the last thing we want to do is spend it with someone we don't like.

Your tribe mates must have mutual respect for each other; find each other interesting; and share similar backgrounds, lifestyles, and values. We all like to associate and do business with people that we like. Creating a community with high-quality individuals provides this kind of opportunity for its members.

There are thousands of communities and events online that are vying for your ICP's attention and time. You want your members to feel that they are part of something … that they are special and that they were selected because they were such a great fit for the community. As well, when you start with the right people, they will inevitably bring people into the community that are of the same caliber as they.

There are people who don't belong in your community. Figuring out who belongs and who doesn't is a huge decision that can affect the overall and long-term success of your community.

3. In-person and live access to you and each other is important

A study conducted by The Economist Intelligence Unit showed that four out of six of the key ingredients for forming strong relationships required in-person interaction. This is important because the members of your community need to interact with each other.

Forming relationships only online by using text to communicate is super hard because there are no emotions, facial expressions, tone of voice, body language, or other non-verbal cues to enhance communication.

Consequently, you need to create opportunities for your tribe members to interact in person and face to face. These opportunities can come in the form of boot camps, seminars, meet and greets, live chat sessions, conferences, etc. By holding these events, you leverage the relationships that have been started online and strengthen them with solid human interaction. Your folks will get to know each other even better and be more conversational with each other at the time of meeting and long after when they're exchanging texts and IMs.

4. It all starts with you

When a community first starts, most people don't know what to do because they have no frame of reference on what's supposed to happen. As a result, your members are going to be looking to you as the leader for what to do how to do it. Additionally, the early seekers in your community have no identity or reputation with the other members, so there's really no impetus for them to speak up or to be a leader themselves.

To that end, you must facilitate and lead the communication efforts of the community in the beginning.

To do this, you'll need to provide examples of how you want the communication to flow, how you want members to treat each other, and what types of interactions you like the best.

When Reddit, one of the largest online communities in the world started to take off, it created fake accounts to create the feel of a larger community and to get people engaged. The strategy is called "astroturfing." Although they weren't transparent with what was going on, it did ensure that there was content and conversation to be consumed while members were active in the community—a crucial element of not only getting the ball rolling, but also keeping it rolling.

One of the strategies that works well is to do question and answer sessions where you, as the leader, field questions from members to get the ball rolling. The communication may start slowly with the awkward period where people don't want to ask questions. Eventually, as one or two questions get asked, more members will step up and start to ask questions.

If you want your members to communicate and add content to your community, you must take the first step and get the interactions going.

5. If it's going to be, it's up to me

No doubt, this is going to take hard work and persistence. You're going to set up live chats, question and answer sessions, webinars, and other online events and nobody is going to show up. Or, you're going to make posts or share content and nobody will comment or respond.

This, friend, is the nature of the beast in building a community. The good news for you is that consistent action doesn't always produce consistent results, but it does produce success.

Any community in existence now is only there because a leader like you decided to not quit and to do everything it takes to make it a reality. As long as you're committed to making it happen, it will happen. Every community that exists today only exists because someone cared enough to bust their ass and make it happen. If you have that drive, nothing else really matters.

People want to be led—there's no question about it. When you add that to the fact that people are naturally drawn to being part of a community that is driven by an effective leader who has a vision and passion they can rally around, you have the recipe for building a throng of loyalists who will do everything they can be part of that group.

It's important to remember that while the community starts with you, it's not about you. It's about the shared values and purpose that you and your community find in common. When those are the right match with the right people, your community has the foundation it needs to be uber successful.

What's most important is that you must lead your community and keep strengthening it by any means necessary until your Promoters and Advocates help carry the baton and start growing the community by reaching people you wouldn't normally reach or to whom you would not have access. It's at this point that your community takes on a life of its own and becomes one of your best content creators and salespeople.

Join our **community on Facebook** at digitalpresident.com/community

CONCLUSION

A natural question to ask at this point would be: "Where do I go from here?" Our hope is that you at least did the exercises in the book that we recommended you complete. If you did, the next steps will be easy for you to complete.

First, you have to determine what you are absolutely dyed-in-the-wool passionate about. Whatever your passion is will drive you to do everything you can to become the Digital President of your corner of the earth. Without passion, there is no fuel to see this through to fruition.

Next, you need to determine your purpose. Your purpose is also known as your "why." Why do you put your feet on the floor every morning and work hard each day to achieve what you achieve?

Your purpose is not your mission statement. Your mission is "what" you plan to do, be, or have as it relates to your life and business. Your purpose is why you do it.

That's an important distinction for sure, and many people miss it.

Lastly, what's your promise? Hopefully, by now, you've figured out what you are the best in the world at doing. If you've done that, then it should be fairly easy for you to come up with your promise in the form of a value proposition that will influence your buyer personas to stand up and pay attention when you talk.

Once you've gotten this figured out, you now need to make sure it all aligns with your Life by Strategy. If you recall, living a Life by Strategy means that you do the work that you love to do while at the same time deriving a tremendous amount of fulfillment from delivering value each day to those with whom you work.

Any misalignment here dampens your results, affecting your ability to live a Life by Strategy and to provide people with the value and outcomes they desire by seeking you out.

To prevent any breakdown here, you'll want to ask yourself the following questions:

- Where am I going to invest my time? – Time holds ultimate value in your life. Be crystal clear on where and when you are going to spend this precious commodity. It's your time, so choose how you use it wisely.
- Where am I going to stop spending time? – Take the time to complete a stop-doing list. What activities are you going to stop investing time in doing? Who do you need to stop spending time with? The sooner you do this, the sooner you'll have more time to allocate to doing the things you want and need to do.
- What am I going to sacrifice so I can buy my time back? – We think this poem from *Think and Grow Rich* captures the essence of what we are saying best:

> I bargained with life for a penny
> and life would pay no more,
> however, I begged at evening
> when I counted my scanty store;
>
> For life is a just employer
> he gives you what you ask
> but, once you have set the wages
> why, you must bear the task;
>
> I worked for a menial's hire
> only to learn dismayed
> that any wage I had asked of life,
> life would have willingly paid.

What task are you "willing to bear" in order to get your time back and live the life you really want and deserve? As with all things worthwhile, there is a sacrifice that needs to be made.

Once you've gotten all of this squared away, you need to figure out who your target market is. Your target market is the group of consumers to whom you are going to market your product and service. It's not just any group of people. It's the people who are going to be impacted the greatest by you and your product and service. It's the people who, once they see and know how you can help them solve their problems, will walk through fire to tell the world about you.

Be sure to do your research and pick the right target market for your message. It will make all the difference in you results.

From here, it's time to put your thinking cap on and figure out what you're the Digital President of. By now, you should be pretty clear on what that is. And if you are, then you are ready to start breaking down your core content and adding value to the people who are already—or are soon to be—members of your community.

If you do all this—even if you don't have a product—amazing things are going to happen in your business and life.

Remember, being Digital President isn't just about your product, it's about you, the value you bring to the table and your ability to change and influence lives while you create an incredible one for yourself.

ABOUT THE AUTHORS

Michael Reese and Woods Davis marketers and entrepreneurs who have generated over 45,000,000 U.S. dollars selling products and services online, spent millions of dollars on marketing campaigns, and run multiple seven figure companies.

CPSIA information can be obtained
at www.ICGtesting.com
Printed in the USA
LVHW08*1035220718
584252LV00001BA/2/P